HIRADO: PRINCE OF PORCELAINS

by Louis Lawrence

with an Introduction by

David Hyatt King

Cover
*A model of a seated shishi, her
mane and tail decorated in
underglaze blue. Meiji period.
Height 24.7 cm*

Library of Congress Cataloging-in-publication data:

Lawrence, Louis, 1949-

   Hirado: Prince of Porcelains / by Louis Lawrence; with an introduction by David Hyatt King

      p. cm. – (Encyclopedia of Japanese Art series)

   Includes bibliographical references and index

   ISBN 1-878-52930-7

   1. Hirado porcelain. I. Title. II. Series.

   NK4399.H57L38 1997   97-31964

   738.2'0952'24–dc21   CIP

Published by Art Media Resources, Ltd., 1507 South Michigan Avenue, Suite 200, Chicago, IL 60605
First published in 1997

Designed by Rosanne Chan. Printed by C A Design
Rm 605–6 Kam Chung Building, 54 Jaffe Road, Wanchai, Hong Kong

Bound and printed in Hong Kong

For M.C.D.C. *who encouraged me*

to start putting pen to paper

and

Susan

who inspired me to finish.

Contents

Author's foreword

My research on this book began many years ago and I have no doubt that in thanking the innumerable people who have contributed to the completion of this project I shall inevitably make omissions. So my first thank you, and apology, goes to those whom I fail to mention. Secondly, without attaching any significance to the order in which they are mentioned, this book would have been considerably less complete without the help of Jessica Ahearn, Richard Barker, Helene Bayeu, Floyd Beckford, Joe Belperio, David Bentliff, Philip Cardeiro, Rosanne Chan, Robin Crighton, Barry Davies, Joe Earle, Kathleen Emerson-Dell, Rupert Faulkner, Irene Finch, Robert Fleischel, Barbara Ford, Matthi Forrer, Paul Freeman, Michael Goedhuis, Gretchen Good, Hollis Goodall, Brian Harkins, Victor Harris, Anne Howard, Oliver Impey, Kenneth and Mary Izzo, Dylan Jackson, Akiyoshi and Sami Kaneda, Eve King, Allan Kurtzman, Eleanor Lewis-Bale, Akira Matsura, Meher McArthur, Joan Mirviss, Natsuo Miyashita, Jeffrey Moy, Toshio Noda, Matt Pia, Clare Pollard, Friedrich Reichel, David and Robert Rote, Max Rutherston, Clifford and Jean Schaefer, Tadashi Setsu, Nick Shaw, Sandy Sheckter, F. S. Shimizu, Tsumugi Shoji, Avelino Silva, Robert Singer, Susan Tucker, Makoto Umezawa, David & Linda Wheatley, Jane Wilkinson, Ming Wilson and Hiram J. Woodward.

Thirdly a special thank you to David Hyatt King, "an original Hirado enthusiast" and author of the introduction to this book.

The spelling of the word Matsura throughout this book differs from the more often used and ancient way of writing the family name Matsuura. The origin of the name is most likely to be from the word "matsuro," meaning a backward area as opposed to the culturally sophisticated capital. Matsura has since come to be written with the characters for pine, matsu, and bay, ura. Consequently, and I include myself among the culprits, many, even Japanese, tend mistakenly to read the name as Matsu-ura.

There are no books in English devoted solely to a chronological history of Hirado and those books on Japanese ceramics as a whole; tend to base their writing about Hirado on repetition of hearsay. On ascertaining that porcelain manufacture began at Mikawachi far earlier than had previously been accepted, I reexamined "the facts" and found much to be erroneous. Consequently I have tried to draw on primary source material as far as possible and have sometimes used documentation not previously known in the West. This includes the Imamura family documents, the records of the Matsura family, The Kyoto Prefectural Museum Report of 1882 on Mikawachi porcelain and the report of the Sasebo City Educational Committee of 1983. I have resisted burdening the text with numerous footnotes or vowel lengthening accents on Japanese words as the book is not aimed solely at an academic audience but also at a more general readership who may be attracted by the pictures of the wonderful porcelain or the charm of the history of Hirado.

To establish early dates for specific pieces of Hirado, often even predating the kiln's currently presumed origin, I have discussed some items in great detail and pursued logical arguments that clarify the relevant points. Merely to have presented theories without discussion would have, quite rightly, attracted scepticism among those who think Hirado to be a product of the 19th century made for export. One of the prime objects of this book is to demonstrate otherwise.

As a dealer involved in long term research, I have found that a combination of collectors, museum personnel and dealers who have provided the information and innovation which turned this book into reality. Without all three there is no doubt that this would not have been possible. Over the years I have encountered some degree of unjustified suspicion among the three groups and I hope that one effect of this publication will be to diminish such feelings. I am certain that progress in the search for new knowledge and information could be aided by a greater co-operation and openness.

Louis Lawrence
October 1997

References in the captions and text to Appendix 6, where marks are shown, are referred to as follows: (app.6, no.55)

The following abbreviations have been used in the text and footnotes when referring to other publications:

AJ   —   *Assignment Japan: von Siebold, Pioneer and Collector* (The Hague,.1989)

Brinkley   —   Brinkley, Captain F., *Japan: Its History Arts and Literature* (Boston, 1901)

Cardeiro   —   Cardeiro, C. Philip, *Hirado Ware* (Monterey, 1989)

Garner   —   Garner, H.M., *Oriental Blue and White* (London, 1954)

Jenyns   —   Jenyns, Soame, *Japanese Porcelain* (London, 1965)

Noda I   —   Noda, Toshio, Dr., *Hizen Hirado yaki Yokohon* (Japan, 1989)

Noda II   —   Noda, Toshio, Dr., *Miwaka no ko-Hirado yaki* (Japan, 1993)

TOCS   —   King, David Hyatt, *Transactions of the Oriental Ceramic Society. "Hirado Porcelain: Its Dating"* (London 1981)

Introduction

This is a welcome, indeed long overdue, book on one of Japan's greatest porcelain factories, which enjoyed enduring princely patronage from the Matsura family, Lords of Hirado Island. We can confidently identify a distinctive Hirado ware from the late 17th century to the 1920's.

Indeed Appendix 3 lists the known dated pieces from 1723 to 1907. The emphasis of Hirado ware was always on fine ceramic art, initially for use either by the family or as gifts. In the 19th century, commercial workshops were installed, making widely varied wares with an increasing proportion for sale at home and abroad. Appendix 7 reprints an extract from a fascinating 1891 Manchester Guardian article, showing the family's significant stake in what had become a company and fine pieces were made up to 1925.

AIMS OF THIS BOOK

They are to display Hirado ware with its subtlety, charm and magnificence in broadly chronological order; to summarise the documentation, and to underpin these with information about Western collectors, and an Appendix (6) with all known Hirado artists' signatures. In my view the author succeeds in his aims; furthermore the details here can be trusted since the author has used over 20 years' enthusiasm and world-wide experience to winnow out the many Hirado imitations.

HIRADO'S REPUTATION—ITS ESSENTIAL QUALITIES

The factory has enjoyed a broadly favourable press, from M. Shioda (ed. Franks) writing for the 1876 Philadelphia Exhibition, to Lawrence Smith in the 1970's. From the colour plates, you may agree that this was a remarkable factory; why has there been no Western book until now? There are various answers which also say a good deal about the factory.

Firstly, Japanese art, especially the later decorative sort, has been unfashionable for much of this century. Secondly, the Japanese have seen themselves as pottery, not porcelain, makers; if they made porcelain, it was early—before 1700, or late—about 1900. This book proves superb pieces were made in every generation, as at Nabeshima—Hirado's implicit rival. Thirdly, Hirado largely avoided such competition by seldom enamelling its wares (but see chapter 6); instead Hirado opted for white, blue and white (and a little underglaze red), and a few high-fired coloured glazes such as celadon. Inevitably, the factory's reputation suffered in the West, where quality ceramics are usually brightly coloured. Fourthly, Hirado—drawing on both Chinese and Korean traditions—concentrated on smaller Japanese tea ceremony wares, such as water jars, censers and flower vases. These are shapes unfamiliar in the West. Finally, Hirado ware is rare, especially before 1850. We therefore see almost everything as later 19th century—an unfashionable period; the remarkable merits of the originals have also been clouded by many copies.

HIRADO'S DEVELOPMENT AND ACHIEVEMENTS

The author presents the case for distinctive mid 17th century Hirado (plates 10, 17 and 22); but he has sensibly opted for the earliest likely date of late 17th century. However the discovery in Japan over the last 20 years of so many dated 18th century pieces, suggests that 17th century dated pieces may be found, to complement the documentation. It is interesting that Oliver Impey's valuable "The Early Porcelain Kilns of Japan" includes as Plate 43c, an Arita dish dated to 1653. If Arita were doing this, possibly Hirado also wrote dates on their porcelains in the mid 17th century.

The 18th century presentation wares are small, simple, greyish and greenish types, long admired for their delicacy (plates 6, 11–13). This pervades their shapes, the milky glaze and the characteristic violet underglaze blue which combine to make evocative use of blank areas. The later 18th century saw general use of a whiter paste, larger shapes and complex designs (plates 24, 26 and 35). Hirado also modelled people, animals and plants. These attractively fuse Japanese preference, Chinese themes and Western influence, either from imported prints and watercolours, or from Okyo's school, (plates 29, 30, 31, 33, 83 & 84). Apart from their use as gifts, these miniatures also serve as vase finials, jar knops and netsuke (plates 26, 42, 68, 80–82). The famous Leiden flower models, made before 1828 (plate 32), show that items are often considerably earlier than we might think.

Output greatly increased in the 19th century, for markets at home and abroad, with varied styles and techniques running concurrently (plates 42, 44, 56, 58–61, 62). Such richness may not be to all tastes, but as in contemporary metal or lacquer work, the level of skill in, for example, sculptural carving or low relief is undeniable (plates 69, 71, 75–78, 86). A minor difference of opinion between the author and myself concerns dating the grandly sculptured later presentation pieces (plates 42, 44, 57, and 58). He says correctly in chapter 4 that 1893 is their earliest firm date and he sees them as all made between 1860 and 90, for export, possibly to China. This cautious good sense is undeniable! Future information may clarify whether the group began 30 or even 60 years earlier.

CONCLUSION

The author illustrates key pieces from public collections, but could have included more, had museums been charging lower reproduction fees. I therefore appeal to museums to moderate their future charges to scholarly enterprises like this. Fortunately, the riches of private collections have allowed excellent coverage. Indeed, the author could have filled another six volumes with equally good pieces, so great was Hirado's achievement.

For over 200 years, Hirado was a subsidised enterprise where—at the higher levels—excellent artists and craftsmen created fine art for enlightened patrons. Hirado's house style is impressively uniform over generations and, especially in the models, filled with surprises and delights. This is a Japanese equivalent to the official Chinese imperial/court porcelains; I hope you come to admire as I do, what the author has given us here.

David Hyatt King

Plate 2

A globular bottle vase with
slender neck painted with
clusters of pine trees beneath
a lappet border. This large
heavy bottle of generous form
has none of the complexities of
Meiji design and dates
from the end of the Edo era.
Height 33.4 cm

The place of the Matsura family in history

Matsura: ancient traditions.

Although there is much controversy over the precise date, it is certain that the first articles made from porcelain in Japan were produced in Arita by 1620. Prior to that date all ceramics produced in Japan were made from opaque material and it was not until clay suitable for making translucent porcelain was discovered within the country's borders that the first porcelain was created. The early history of the beginnings of Japan's ceramic production is steeped in legend and such is the lack of primary source information that it will remain a subject of speculation for years to come.

For us to have any sensible idea about ceramic production at that time we must look closely at contemporary life in Japan, its traditions, its history as well as its economic and artistic status. Initially it may seem fortunate that this era is well documented and recorded. It is the era of Nobunaga, Hideyoshi and Tokugawa. In fact the famous siege of Osaka castle that finally established the Tokugawa shogunate and began the long era of lasting peace took place in 1615. It would be easy to assume that for such exciting times in Japan, records would give us a clear picture of almost every aspect of life there and in fact one could not ask for better documentation or references. The 20th century too has added to our understanding of the Japan of this time by the production of books and films that accurately document the era, recreating period costume and dwellings and giving an insight into both court and peasant lifestyles.

The early history of the Matsura family and of the establishment of the Hirado kilns has been pieced together by referring to old documents from the Matsura and Imamura families. It is astonishing that we are know so much of such ancient families and enterprises and yet when we move into the 18th century, the picture becomes less clear. One important documented event that had a significant effect on the kilns was the reorganisation of the system of kilns run by the clan in 1759. The effect was to expand production at the Mikawachi kilns by relocating workers from other areas.

The porcelain industry started in Kyushu and to this day maintains its centre there. Kyushu is the most southerly and westerly of Japan's three major islands and Arita, the location of the first porcelain kilns, is in the north western segment of the island some 600 km from Kyoto as the crow flies. This distance, in an age before modern transport, meant that the conflicts and politics of the mainland had a very different effect from nowadays on the population. The fact that the two large islands were separated by water compounded the situation and made it yet more difficult for interaction. It was not that the politics of the mainland were completely irrelevant to Kyushu but that the influences were largely imposed from a distance. The central figures and families maintained power on the island and this power was harnessed by the central rulers of Japan by alliances and treaties rather than by battles and wars. This meant that the people of Kyushu were able, to some extent, to develop their own characteristics and culture differently from those on the main island of Honshu.

To get a clear picture of life in Kyushu at the beginning of the 17th century we must look at the most influential and powerful families. At the south westerly corner of the island the Shimazu family ruled Satsuma province. They were wealthy and powerful, to a large extent because of their trading links with the more southerly Ryuku Islands, Japan's major source of sugar. Over centuries the Shimazu were politically active, a constant powerful force that only diminished after the Meiji Restoration in 1868. In fact they were one of the main catalysts that led finally to the abolition of the shogunal system in Japan. Another powerful family on Kyushu was the Matsura. They can trace their origins back as far as the Heian period when in 822 Minamoto-no Toru was the 18th son born to the Emperor Saga. He served the Imperial family in Kyoto, living in Kawara and becoming known as the Kawara minister of the Left. Minamoto-no Toru's son followed in his father's footsteps as a civil servant but his grandson became a warrior and in so doing changed the course of the family's history. From that date on until recent history, all heads of the family were warriors, Watanabe-no Tsuna, the fifth generation, becoming particularly noteworthy as a fierce combatant and still remembered as one of the famous generals of Minamoto-no Yoritomo, the first Kamakura shogun. It was Watanabe-no Tsuna who became the first member of the family to set foot on Kyushu when he was sent to suppress a rebellion in the latter part of the 10th century. A later descendant, Minamoto Hisashi, the eighth generation who lived from 1064 to 1148, was appointed military governor of the domains of Matsura, Sonogi and Iki on Kyushu and it was he who truly first established the family on this westerly isle. He changed his name to Matsura Hisashi after the location and also adopted the mulberry leaf (kaji) as a family crest (mon) in addition to the three stars that Minamoto-no Toru had originally chosen as his family emblem.

Matsura Hisashi was the first of his family to build a castle on Kyushu but it was not until the eleventh generation that Matsura Tamotsu established himself on Hirado Island in 1225, erecting a castle on the site that was to become the seat of the Matsura family for the next 700 years. The domain he ruled was larger than the island of Hirado itself and extended almost as far east as the town of Arita and as far south as Amakusa Island.

The establishment of a well-fortified and secure headquarters did not mean that the Matsura family was without conflicts and troubles. At that time territorial borders had to be protected from neighbouring daimyo and confrontations were frequent for the next 200 years. That the Matsura clan was a powerful and important force in Japan is shown by its key involvement in protecting the country from foreign invaders. In 1274 the leaders of the Yuan dynasty in China founded by the Mongol Kubilai Khan assembled a huge army of Chinese, Mongol and Korean troops to invade Japan, first landing on the small island of Iki and proceeding to Hakata (present day Fukuoka City). The Matsura daimyo was active in assembling a force to repel the invaders, leading an army of his own and other local soldiers over 100 km to confront the enemy, finally forcing them to retreat.

Plate 3
Hirado castle, Hirado Island.

Plate 4
*A portrait of Matsura Hisanobu,
(1571–1602), painted by
Katayama Shokei, the Matsura
official court painter,
inscribed and dated 1684 by
Denshin Sotei.*

20

The coup de grace was fortuitously assisted by a sudden storm that wrecked many of the invaders' ships. The storm, known as kamikaze (holy wind) became legendary, and is considered to have been sent by the gods to rescue Japan. Another similar invasion was attempted in 1281 but the daimyo of Kyushu had made preparations to thwart further attacks by building fortified defences and the intruders from the mainland were quickly forced to retreat. Even though both these conflicts were largely outside the domain of the Matsura clan, the family played a leading role in this defence of their country.

This is not to say that war was a constant concern. There were long intervals of peace and during these times the Matsura domain prospered. In 1191 the famous monk Eisai returned from his travels in China to establish himself on Hirado Island. He was the first to introduce Zen Buddhism to Japan and established a temple there. Although the temple itself was destroyed soon after Eisai's death and not rebuilt until 1695, many esteemed Buddhist monks from China visited Hirado on their way to the mainland. Apart from Zen Buddhism, Eisai was also the first to introduce the cultivation of tea to Japan. He became acquainted with the beverage on his visit to China and returned with seeds which he planted. The importance of tea in almost every aspect of Japanese life cannot be underestimated and it is fitting that its first contact should have been in Hirado because, in later years tea was a driving force behind the establishment of the Hirado kilns and the inspiration for many of its products.

It is clear that Hirado Island was not only an important military centre but also a spiritual one. The means to support this power base and further establish the clan as truly influential could not have come solely from the stipend provided by the shogun. It is well known that the Tokugawa shogunate isolated Japan from western world both culturally and economically and all too often it's forgotten that previously there was an active and sizable trade with China and other neighbouring countries.

Hirado, being geographically one of the closest provinces to the mainland, was best placed to take advantage of trade opportunities and the natural harbour on the island was an additional asset put to good use. From as early as the 12th century, trade links were established with lands that have now become known as the Philippines, Vietnam, Thailand, Malaysia, as well as China itself. Over the centuries the Matsura clan accumulated wealth through these trading relationships and this enabled them to become a dominant force both militarily and politically in northern Kyushu. It was not until the mid 16th century that the first Europeans landed in Japan hoping to establish trading links. The Portuguese were the first to arrive, followed by the Spanish, Dutch and English and although they traded with several daimyo whose lands were situated on the west coast of Kyushu, all the Europeans operated to some extent through Hirado. By allowing missionaries to settle and practise, Matsura Takanobu (1529–1599) greatly increased the profits that could be reaped from trade with the Europeans and the family's coffers were increased by the import duties he imposed. However it was not only trade that benefited the Japanese. The introduction of firearms was an important contribution to increasing the military strength of those already in power: the Matsura daimyo soon learnt how to use these new weapons and quickly discovered how to make an arsenal, casting cannon and matchlock rifles in iron.

By the 16th century the Matsura were in their prime, a situation they enjoyed for the next two hundred years. From 1560 sporadic provincial warfare gave way to large-scale campaigns between Nobunaga, Tokugawa and their allies as these factions struggled to become the supreme leaders of the entire nation. Nobunaga was gaining the upper hand but before he could consolidate his conquest, he was assassinated in 1582. Hideyoshi hunted down the assailant and then continued his conquest of Kyushu. His vastly superior armies forced the opposing daimyos to yield and Matsura Shigenobu (1549–1614) was persuaded to join with Hideyoshi in a campaign against the southernmost daimyo, Shimazu of Satsuma who soon capitulated. Having become the effective ruler of all Japan, he decide to invade Korea and it was to Shigenobu that he turned for help. Shigenobu provided detailed maps of Korea and was later summoned to Osaka to join in the discussions prior to an invasion. He was appointed to organise the assembly of a fleet to initiate the invasion. It was no small task and a year later a force of some 300,000 men set out for Korea. Not only was Shigenobu one of Hideyoshi's leading generals, he also provided a garrison of troops from Hirado that captured over 4,800 of the enemy. Although there was a period of peace in 1596 and the majority of the generals returned to their homes. Shigenobu stayed in Korea to supervise the forces that remained, returning only at the end of the campaign in 1598 when Hideyoshi died.

In the years after Hideyoshi's death large-scale warfare returned to the country. Fortunately it centred around the major cities of Honshu, so the destruction that warfare brings did not touch the populace of the western island. The campaigns were finally concluded in 1615 with Tokugawa Ieyasu's victory over the Toyotomi clan at Osaka. The long-standing peace that followed saw the Matsura in an enviable position. Wealthy, powerful and situated far enough away from the centres of the courts to avoid becoming entirely involved in the incessant and debilitating games of politics, they enjoyed the fruits of their forebears' labours. Indeed Matsura Shigenobu and Tokugawa Ieyasu had already entered into an alliance in 1601, confirming the status and strength of the Hirado fiefdom.

So after a long campaign abroad, Shigenobu returned home a proud and wealthy daimyo untroubled by his neighbours and safe in the knowledge that he had the support of the most powerful leader in the land. Like many of the other generals away on the campaign in Korea, he had been in contact with the arts and crafts of the country they were attempting to conquer. Again like his contemporaries, he brought back many of the craftsmen to create their wares in his homeland.

It was the potters who held the greatest fascination for the Japanese and several arrived in Japan to settle in the latter years of the campaign. Some were brought against their will. Others, probably because they had formed alliances with the invaders and would find it difficult to remain in their homeland without severe persecution, emigrated voluntarily. These potters were able to produce a wide range of ceramics both decorated and undecorated in pottery as they had done for centuries in their homeland.

The Kyushu daimyos soon installed these potters within the boundaries of their domains, providing them with all they needed to begin making pottery. They used local clays which were most suitable for making Karatsu type wares. These were produced at a variety of kilns and so their characteristics differ greatly. Most typical are those with a coarse brown body overlaid with a whitish slip glaze and painted in brown oxide with designs of grasses, reeds, grapes, wisteria and geometric patterns. In form and design they are close to wares of the Korean Yi dynasty and are executed in a free and spontaneous style which marks the beginning of a characteristic Japanese style and spirit.

The first knowledge of the making of pottery on the lands of the Matsura fief is in 1598 when the potters that Shigenobu had sent back established a kiln on Hirado Island itself at a site named Nakano. The products made here until its closure in 1650 came to be known as Nakano ware. These are made from local clay which fires to a light cream colour. They are often painted in underglaze blue and covered with a whitish glaze which displays an even, crackled pattern. The motifs used in decorating these earliest Hirado products include landscapes (plate 5), flowers, bamboo, grasses, willow, camellia, tigers and ho-o birds. The shapes that have been recorded are all utilitarian—tea bowls, small dishes, sake bottles and water jars. The founding potter was Koseki Tonroku who set up residence with his wife Koraiba and their son Nakazato Shige'emon. Koseki was given the art name Imamura Yajibei and Imamura became a

Plate 5
A Nakano water jar of ogee
form painted with landscape.
This 17th century jar clearly
shows the crackle in the glaze
so characteristic of pieces made
at Nakano on Hirado Island.
Height 19.0 cm

name that is found in connection with Hirado wares from these very first days until their demise in the 20th century. The partnership between the Matsura and Imamura families remained unbroken for three hundred years and created some of the most outstanding ceramics ever made.

Along with other Korean potters working throughout western Kyushu they were successfully producing pottery with local clays that were easily available to them. They were as yet unable to produce the treasured porcelain that the Chinese had been making for centuries. The raw material was simply not available and so the search began for a suitable clay. Legend has it that the first to discover clay suitable for making porcelain was Ri Sampei who dug into the mountain at Izumiyama in 1614 to find a vast treasure of kaolin clay. Whether it was truly the legendary Ri Sampei or another of his contemporaries and whether the date is precisely correct or not is unknown. What is certain is that the first true porcelain was being created in Japan from the early 1620's.

Ri Sampei established his kiln close to the source of his good fortune at the base of Izumiyama at Arita and the porcelain production centre of Japan was born. Being outside the Matsura fief's borders but in the Nabeshima daimyo's domain, the Hirado potters had no access to this source of porcelain clay and so continued to search for their own supply.

The search for fine clay was not the only event in Hirado or Kyushu that was of concern and importance to the population in the early years of the 17th century. Christianity, which had been introduced by the Spanish and was beginning to find favour with some Japanese particularly in Hirado, was banned and severe religious persecution followed. The now fabled ship's pilot Will Adams was shipwrecked on the coast of Bungo Prefecture. He became an influential figure at the court of Tokugawa Ieyasu but maintained a home on Hirado Island. It is said that he flew the Union flag from his roof when in residence! Both the Dutch (in 1609) and the English (in 1613) established trading posts in Hirado. Though it seemed the trading traditions of the Matsura were to continue with new partners, this turned out to be a short-lived affair. After the famous battle of Sekigahara that finally consolidated Tokugawa Ieyasu's political control, he issued edicts that began to close Japan's borders and restricted trade with foreigners solely to the ports of Nagasaki and Hirado. The Spanish were expelled entirely in 1624, mainly due to their aggressive missionary activities. The presence of the English was short-lived and they closed their trading post in 1623 due to lack of commercial success; instead of offering products that had a ready market with the Japanese such as sugar, spices, skins and silks, as other European traders did, the English, in spite of advice from their leader Richard Cocks, chose to promote typically British products such as wool and other fabrics which were not popular and unsuited to the climate. The Dutch were more successful and maintained their base on Hirado island until forced to move in 1640.

Records show that a kiln was first opened at Mikawachi in 1622, and this small village became the centre of production for the fine porcelain known as Hirado. Although over 60 km from Hirado Island it was located less than 5 km from Arita and yet within the borders of the Hirado fief. It was eminently suitable because in that same year a good quality clay[1] was discovered nearby, though its high iron content left traces of red on unglazed areas and it tended to turn the glaze a blue-grey colour. By now the leadership of the Matsura clan had fallen to Shigenobu's grandson Takanobu and it must have been under his instruction that the first steps in establishing the famous group of kilns was initiated.

This was not the only kiln that operated within the borders of the fief. In the coming years 31 kilns were in operation at various times (see appendix 2) and although the wares produced are not typical of what has become known as Hirado porcelain, they are nevertheless Hirado products in a more general sense. There is a vase of stoneware verging on porcelain in the collection of Tsuragamine Castle Museum, on Hirado island inscribed in underglaze blue, 10th year of Genwa (1624) made by Oyomada Sakei. It is reputed to come from the Enaga kiln, at Kihara[2]. This demonstrates that ceramics were being made in Hirado at this date and it is likely that attempts to make porcelain were being carried out.

The porcelain clays used by all the potters in the general area of Arita were all chemically similar. The artistic influences on all the groups of potters and decorators were also the same: they were making objects for the same purpose for use by the same class of people. Excavations at the earliest Arita kiln sites have shown several types of slightly greyish porcelain decorated in underglaze blue with motifs that include landscapes,

[1] *Referred to as 'ajiro-tsuchi' in Japan.*

[2] *Kihara is very close to Mikawachi and it is likely clay from that site was used in the production of this vase.*

flowers (both stylised and naturalistic), animals and dragons, as well as geometric patterns and calligraphy. These Arita ceramics from the time before exports to Europe have become known as Shoki Imari.

The possibilities for archaeological research at Mikawachi are entirely different. These major kiln sites are buried under modern housing and are unavailable for excavation. As a result we can only speculate as to the nature of the wares of these first Mikawachi potters. However it is likely that there was very little difference between the types of ceramics made at these two areas in the early years, particularly as the Mikawachi clay closely resembles that seen in the greyish wares of their neighbours. There is no logical reason why there should be any major difference and it is to be hoped that future discoveries may prove or disprove this. New information may well show that some Shoki Imari pieces were in fact made at Mikawachi. This suggestion is supported by the recorded fact that several workers from the Nakano kiln left to join Ri Sampei's workshops in the mid-1620's.

In the ensuing years many other famous kilns were founded in Arita. The best known family, Kakiemon, established a muffle kiln to decorate porcelain with overglaze enamel colours at Nangawara and then a porcelain manufacturing kiln. It is claimed that in 1634 a kiln was established at Iwayakawachi that was later to become the first Nabeshima kiln. In 1637, Matsura Takanobu decided to build a country villa in Mikawachi and at the same time establish a centre of porcelain production to make items for use by members of his family. He ordered Imamura Yajibei's son, Imamura Sannojo, to move from Nakano to Mikawachi and establish a kiln that was to be called The Mikawachi Nagahayama Official Kiln. Production at Nakano quickly diminished. Sannojo was the supervisor (torodaikan) and from the outset he invited potters from nearby kilns that made Karatsu-style wares to participate. He also sought the help of painters to decorate these wares. Among those who became involved from the beginning were Yamanouchi Chobei, an artist from Heianjo Castle in Yamajiro Province, Maeda Tokuemon, an artist from Sasayama in Tamba Province and the potters Nakazato Jiuemon, Fukumoto Yajiemon, Kanejita Soemon and Fujimoto Jiuemon. It is fortunate that the records of these participants still exist. It suggests that the kiln was of a significant size, and in fact is reputed to have had an organisation far superior to other Kyushu kilns. Later in the year, before this new venture could bear fruit, Matsura Takanobu died and was succeeded by his young son Chinshin.

Plate 6

A globular bottle vase with slender neck painted with chrysanthemums against a trellis, the reverse with bell flowers and grasses, all beneath lappet and ruyi borders. The feel and colour of the glaze and the style of decoration closely parallel the set of dishes dated 1723 and this bottle must have been made close to that date. Height 22 cm

Matsura Chinshin establishes the kilns

Only 15 years old, the young Chinshin was the 29th generation of the Matsura family steeped in the traditions of a proud and aristocratic family. Among the most powerful and wealthy men on all Kyushu, he was fortunate to be at the dawn of an era of peace and stability that radically altered every aspect of life in Japan. Rather than being the peace before the storm, this was the quiet before the peace. This is not to say that the new incumbent had no difficulties to handle.

In 1637 the Shimabara Uprising erupted in the neighbouring fief, led by a young man called Amakusa Shiro Tokisada, who thought he was the reincarnation of Jesus Christ. Though his followers were mostly Japanese converts who wanted to protest about the central government's treatment of Christians, their ranks were swelled by others who were equally dissatisfied with the oppressive taxation policies of the daimyo of Shimabara. The insurgents took over and fortified themselves in the castle of Shimabara, waving flags decorated with crosses and holding out against a significantly larger number of professional soldiers sent from neighbouring fiefs, including Hirado. During the siege the Dutch were asked to use their ship's cannon against the rebels. To keep their favoured position at court and protect their trading status, the Dutch acceded to this request and fired at the walls of the castle, though with little effect. The castle finally fell when hunger and thirst began to take their toll. This uprising made the shogun suspicious of all Christian activities and he expelled all Portuguese and cut off diplomatic relations with them.

Only three years later, Tokugawa Iemitsu, still deeply suspicious of all foreigners, investigated the remaining foreign presence in Japan. Although uninvolved in any religious activity, the Dutch trading post at Hirado was found to be strongly fortified and using the excuse that the buildings were marked with a Christian date, "A.D. 1640" Iemitsu ordered them closed immediately and relocated to the small island of Deshima within the port of Nagasaki. This was a significant financial loss to the Matsura clan as they could no longer benefit from the growing

Chinshin: first beginnings.

trade with the Dutch; the taxes would now go directly to the coffers of the central government.

Aside from these difficulties early in Chinshin's tenure there was little to trouble the young leader who had only to manage his lands and people and enjoy the privileges of his court. He quickly gained a reputation as a skilled diplomat and became highly respected for his expertise in both domestic and foreign affairs. With a clear picture of the situation in the mid 17th century in Hirado and more generally in Kyushu, as well as in central Japan, it is easier to understand why the kilns that were to become so famous evolved as they did and not along the lines of the many commercial production centres.

Matsura Chinshin's principal residence was a well fortified castle overlooking the bay on Hirado Island, though he had others, including the villa at Mikawachi, which his father had just begun to construct. His headquarters consisted of a large complex of buildings, the major ones stone-built, others constructed in wood, housing the members of his immediate family, his retainers, advisers and a large garrison of samurai. A daimyo of his standing would need a very large retinue for his protection and to help manage the affairs of his lands. Although one could not say that it was a life 20th century comfort and ease, he lived at a high standard. In common with other daimyo residences, his quarters would have been decorated with fine brocades, painted screens and doors to lighten the effects of the giant blocks of grey stone walls. The objects and scroll paintings were not displayed in quantity as would have been the case in a European palace, but carefully placed individually to reflect the month or season. The Matsura family's position as a major trading partner with many foreign nations must have brought a very interesting array of items and they possessed large collections of such works of art. Among these was a large collection of Chinese porcelain which was sold in the first part of this century[1]. The Matsura fully appreciated the merits of fine Chinese porcelain and the esteem in which it was held motivated the search for

[1] *Two major auction took place at Tokyo Bijitus Club in 1928 and 1935*

kaolin clay within the fief. Since trade with westerners had been reduced to a trickle by the shogun's ban on contact with the outside world culminating in the final forced move of the Dutch to Deshima island in 1640, there was no longer any means of obtaining further pieces of porcelain. This must have increased the desire of the ceramicists to create true porcelain in the Chinese manner. Although a small group of Chinese traders was allowed to build a compound next to the Dutch trading post on Deshima Island in Nagasaki harbour, they too were stringently policed and allowed only to import small quantities of goods. Any fine Chinese ceramics that were imported were likely to be destined for the shogun's court in Edo (now Tokyo), as he maintained direct control of all trade through Nagasaki.

The best efforts of the 17th century Japanese potters generally fell short of the high technical quality of the Chinese porcelains made during the late Ming dynasty and Transitional period. They remained unable to achieve the fine whiteness of body and brightness of underglaze blue that their mainland neighbours had created. The development of pottery on the other hand, had significantly progressed from rough objects made solely for utilitarian purposes to a recognised art form. It was the introduction of the potters from Korea that enabled this to happen. Their skills and experience were such that the developments took place in a comparatively short space of time.

Much of the inspiration for these developments came from Hideyoshi himself. Hideyoshi was an inveterate patron of the arts who quickly realised the power of art as a political tool and skilfully exploited it as an adjunct to his power. Along with other daimyo and several leading merchants of the time, he developed a great interest in the tea ceremony. Realising its potential, he took advantage of the tea ceremony to promote his own interests, encouraging others to participate. He gave tea utensils as rewards for service and lavishly patronised the famous tea master Sen no Rikyu, who in return instructed him in the ways of tea, introducing him to the aesthetic of the diminutive

Plate 7

Samples of clay from Izumiyama (left) and Amakusa Island (right) clearly showing that even in the raw state these two clays were of a different texture and hue.

Plate 8

A sumi-e painting of Hotei and children by Katayama Shokei. Late 17th century.

tearooms, simple utensils and the spirit of humble poverty (wabi)
deliberately attained.

The utensils employed at such ceremonies were
generally made from simple materials and were not lavishly
decorated or embellished. Pottery played an important role in the
tea ceremony, being used for such items as water jars (mizuzashi),
incense boxes (kogo), incense burners (koro), tea caddies (chaire)
and most importantly the tea bowls themselves (chawan). The
preference was for simple restrained pottery in muted colours,
initially based on Korean and Chinese originals. These concepts
were developed and formalised extensively, they were taught by
tea masters who soon sought out native types of pottery that had
attained a distinctly Japanese characteristic. The use of articles
made from porcelain was not extensive, the exception to this
being fine Ming period blue and white porcelain from China,
which was highly regarded, and to a much lesser extent, Shoki
Imari wares.

Hideyoshi's patronage made the tea masters into
lasting representatives of a cultural ideal which was protected
from the ravages of self-conscious sophistication, so maintaining
the natural qualities of rural charm and spontaneity. It was the
subtle irregularities of shape and the nuances of the fall of
the glaze, whether deliberate or accidental, that appealed to the
followers of tea. Hideyoshi's fascination with the tea ceremony
was continued with equal enthusiasm by Tokugawa Ieyasu and
his descendants. It became essential for a daimyo to become
familiar with every aspect of tea as no daimyo could afford to be
ignorant of the correct etiquette. Daimyo competed in the elegant
simplicity of their tearooms and gardens, in their collections of
tea utensils and in demonstrating their skill in entertaining at tea.
This national involvement of almost every daimyo provided an
essential stimulus for a wide variety of craftsmen and artists.
For the potters, this new involvement by the aristocracy and their
followers established pottery as a high art form, elevating it from
a simple utilitarian craft.

Chinshin, who had continued Takanobu's work in establishing the kiln at Mikawachi when the latter died within a year of its inception, was not alone in patronising a kiln. Several other daimyo were equally committed to such pursuits. In 1650 Chinshin authorised the displacement of the last Nakano potters, moving them to join those already working at Mikawachi. The now larger venture was renamed The Hirado Prefecture Official Kiln. Hirado potters, like those from other fiefs were continuing their search for finer, purer clay. It was in 1662, an important turning point for the Mikawachi craftsmen, that a new source of clay was discovered within the borders of the fief on Amakusa Island, some 90 kilometres from Mikawachi by Imamura Yajibei, the grandson of the Nakano potter of the same name.

This clay proved an ideal medium for the potters and in years to come established their wares among the first rank of porcelains from any country. The clay was of a whiter colour than that from Izumiyama and almost entirely free from gritty particles. It was fine, malleable and plastic when worked. Experimentation at Mikawachi showed that the best results were obtained when the clay was combined with local clay, resulting in *a porcelain pate of exceptional fineness and purity.*[2] J.J. Rein was one of the few Westerners to visit Amakusa in the 19th century and he wrote extensively about his visit in the spring of 1875. "Porcelain stone appears on this sterile island, with its slate and sandstone rock, partly in great masses, standing often alone, but generally surrounded with yellowish or grey-white clay sandstone. It is a metamorphic, volcanic rock, white grey-white or yellowish in colour, similar to Arita-ishi but firmer, harder and heavier, and is partly silicated and partly kaolinized. The body presents a fine-grained mass of kaolin and quartz, and contains single quartz grains as well as crystalline hollow spaces from which common feldspar or plagioklas crystals have crumbled away. G. vom Rath found on the walls of these spaces and on small clefts and corners, infinitesimally small splinters of iron mica and apparently new-formed little quartz crystals. These little crystal-shaped cavities are seen in every specimen and are

[2] *Brinkley*

therefore the most striking marks for the recognition and distinction of the Amakusa stone. This rock contains a large portion of potash as may be seen in the analysis of C. Sarnow [see appendix 5]."

The discovery of clay at Amakusa created certain difficulties. The cost of transportation was enormous. Firstly it had to be dug from the ground, transported to boats and loaded, the journey across the sea was next, it was then unloaded and finally transported the next 10 kilometres by cart across the rough terrain to Mikawachi. Even then the process had not finished, as like all untouched clays it had to be purified by sedimentation, yet another time-consuming and labour-intensive process. It is said that after purification only 6% of the clay was used.

Little is known about production in the first few years, though the first Mikawachi kiln remained open until 1668. As already stated, the kiln probably made blue and white wares in the same vein as those produced at nearby Arita. Much experimentation with the newly discovered clay was carried out and no doubt the whiteness of the wares showed marked improvement.

The reason for the kiln's closing was entirely positive; new and bigger kilns and workshops were opened by Chinshin only a very short distance away still within the borders of the township of Mikawachi. The Mikawachi Higashi (east) Kiln was the centre of Hirado production for the next 250 years until it eventually closed in the early Showa period. Other kilns were operating during this long time but the East kiln was the biggest and most important of the production centres. The establishment of this new venture was researched and planned in fine detail, with an official body of administrators appointed to take overall responsibility for the management of the operation. The various roles within the organisation were clearly defined. Both the official Hirado court artists, Katayama Shokei and Katayama Shoshun, were consulted in this process.

Katayama Shokei was the most renowned of the painters employed by the Matsura family. He was born in 1628 and became the adopted son of Yamanouchi Chobee, the first painter to be appointed to the Hirado court as an official artist. In 1630, Kano Naonobu had been given an estate in Edo by the shogun Tokugawa Hidetata, where he founded the Kobikicho branch of the Kano school. It was under this great master's instruction that Katayama Shokei learnt his skill and became known as one of his four great pupils. After his apprenticeship, Matsura Chinshin appointed him official court artist. Later he was sent to Kyoto where he was recognised by the Emperor and given the title of hokkyo[3]. Subsequently he was commissioned to paint scrolls and screens in the Imperial palace. Returning to Hirado after this project was completed, Katayama Shokei lived out his final years in the place where he had spent the majority of his working life and died at the age of 90. His given name was Chikanobu, but he was popularly known as Yahei; his art names were Ganunsai and Shokei.

Katayama Shoshun was Shokei's younger brother and he too was adopted by Yamanouchi Chobee, following both his brother and father as official artist to the Hirado court and like them given the rank of hokkyo.

It is clear that Matsura Chinshin was intimately involved with the arts throughout his life. He himself gained a reputation as a poet but his interests extended much further than the literary arts. His enthusiasm for the tea ceremony led him to found his own school in 1685, the Chinshin-ryu. This style of tea ceremony became known as the "warrior's tea ceremony" and was often practised among samurai. It was developed by Chinshin himself and was loosely based on that of another daimyo, Katagiri Sekishu. Chinshin wrote, "Martial arts and cultural pursuits are the two main areas of activity a warrior should pursue. The tea ceremony therefore must be performed with an elegance befitting a military lord. It must be a powerful elegance, not frail. Tea must be a route toward disciplining the

[3] Hokkyo, literally "bridge of the law" was the lowest honorary rank given by an Emperor, initially to priests, then subsequently to Buddhist sculptors and later still to painters.

Plate 9

A rice bowl painted with three hollyhock (aoi) mon of the Tokugawa clan. This bowl was part of a set made in the early 18th century and was probably part of a gift presented on one of the daimyo's biannual visits to Tokyo. Diameter 10.3 cm

spirit." This school is still maintained today and is actively led and promoted by Matsura Akira, the 41st generation of the Matsura family.

Chinshin the poet, Chinshin the master of tea ceremony and Chinshin the patron of artists; all these indicate a highly cultured man with a deep appreciation and understanding of the arts. Many of Katayama Shokei's paintings have been inscribed by Chinshin, indicating the daimyo's close and direct involvement with the painter himself. There can be no doubt that Chinshin took a close interest in the progress of his kilns. The wares made at the kilns would have been used by him, his family and his court both as everyday utensils and during the tea ceremony. The selection of utensils for the tea ceremony was highly personal, each item was chosen to reflect the mood or communicate the atmosphere the host required and so any utensils chosen by him would have been cherished and personally appreciated.

HIRADO: PRINCE OF PORCELAINS

The Japanese custom of giving presents when visiting guests at all social levels provided the wealthy Matsura family with a unique opportunity to demonstrate the fine wares of the Hirado kilns. Although several daimyo throughout Japan were connected to pottery kilns by patronage and could command items to be made for gifts when required, there were only two kilns making porcelain whose products were the exclusive property of their patrons These were the Nabeshima and Hirado kilns. Neither of these two daimyo had at that time any commercial interest in promoting their products and they never offered them for sale. It is said that the Nabeshima daimyo had moved his kiln from Iwayakawachi and had established a new base at Okawachi to produce blue and white, celadon and overglaze enamelled polychrome wares. The vast majority of these distinctive products, often decorated with bold asymmetric designs were medium-sized dishes which have gained an international reputation for the spectacular individuality of their design, their quality and their rarity. To have been able to present a visiting daimyo, the Emperor or shogun with fine and unique products from one's own exclusive porcelain kiln must have given these two daimyos a kudos and status that was unattainable by their counterparts. Certainly the reputation of Hirado wares must have benefited greatly from this prestigious position.

As was the case with their neighbours at Arita, the latter part of the 17th century saw big improvements in the quality of porcelain made by the Kyushu potters through technical changes. The Mikawachi kilns began to use a primary firing while the wares were still unglazed rather than leaving them to bake in the sun to dry the moisture from the clay naturally. This change significantly reduced losses in the kilns and is said to have improved the whiteness of the paste. The Arita kilns made small items made for use in Japan from the first years of the 18th century to almost the middle of the century are sometimes referred to as "prime period Imari". They typify the height of achievement attained in making underglaze blue decorated wares

and are well represented in "Beauty of Prime Period Imari" by
Mr K. Seki. (Japan, 1990)

A petition drawn up in 1698 lists Katayama Shoshun
and Shikata Sagouemon, both official court artists, among others
who were involved in the working of the kilns; another sure
indication that painters were involved in ceramic production.
In addition to the seven individuals mentioned, it also names five
other families who were employed at the kilns, giving an idea of
the scale of works at the site at this time.

In 1699 Matsura Chinshin gave a special order for
pieces that he could present to the Imperial Court in Kyoto and
at the same time he honoured Imamura Yajibei with the title of
Higashi Honganji. Obviously a personal reference to the qualities
of the man himself; "higashi" means "east" and refers to the name
and site of the kiln; "honganji" means "monkey-like". In 1703,
at the age of 82, Chinshin died at the same time as the last trickle
of wares from the Nakano kilns ceased. During his life time
Chinshin played a significant part in consolidating the era of
peace that was to last for almost two more centuries. Both
nationally and within his own domain, he was a highly regarded
figure. The impact of the tea ceremony artistically, culturally and
even politically was a most important institution at the time
he was alive and he founded a new and respected school of tea.
He was a major instigator of the creation of the porcelain industry
in Japan; though Hirado may currently be regarded as a fine but
minor product, history may change this view. We may come to
appreciate that Hirado and the Matsura family played an
important role in the development of the industry as a whole.
The accomplishments of Matsura Chinshin cannot be
overestimated.

Plate 10

A moulded octagonal sake bottle painted with rugged landscape. Distinctly flawed in its manufacture this late 17th century piece was painted by Katayama Shokei or one of his followers. This rare group of bottles are among the earliest porcelains made at Mikawachi and although landscapes became a popular subject for the decorators in later years they were never able to recreate the vibrant spontaneity of the painting on these first examples. Height 16.5 cm

Hirado in the 18th century

The outline of the early history of the Matsura family is relatively easy to establish and it is not difficult to demonstrate that Mikawachi was the centre of porcelain production at the dates already stated. However, to establish the precise nature of the production at any specific time presents more difficulties. Nevertheless records may show that a particular artist or potter was appointed at a known date, or that production increased, or changed its nature and this is certainly a great help in understanding Hirado. But there are no photographs, no drawings or sketches to establish exactly what they made until the latter part of the 19th century. We have to rely a few firm pointers; pieces with dated inscriptions, boxes with dedications and use careful detective work to determine a reasoned chronology that is logical and demonstrably accurate. Having established dates of specific pieces, these can then be used to plot a chronology that gives a clear picture of production, as affected and changed by influences in the world outside the parameters of the kiln itself.

As already suggested the first products of the Mikawachi kilns were probably similar to Shoki Imari. There is a problem in ascertaining precisely what wares were made after these early times. Examples of 17th and 18th century Hirado wares are rare, particularly in the West. By comparing these with other similar or related porcelains in collections worldwide, we are able to establish a chronology that gives a clearer picture of the evolution of the kilns. While doing this it is also important to look at the work of other kilns at this time and take particular note of the products of their very near neighbours, the Arita potters.

Pieces inscribed with 19th century dates or otherwise datable are relatively common, but none bearing 17th century inscriptions, apart from the very early 1624 Enaga vase mentioned on page 27, have yet been discovered. Datable pieces from the 18th century are still extremely rare: only seven examples are known. The earliest of these is a set of small dishes (plates 11 & 12) measuring 14.25 cms painted with wild chrysanthemum and

Mikawachi: the golden era.

Plate 11

One of a set of five small dishes painted with chrysanthemum sprays, the reverse with scrolling branches of peaches and curled tendrils; the inscription dates the piece to 1723. This important set of dishes firmly establish the fact that the Hirado kilns were already making fine porcelain of high quality by this date. Diameter 14.25 cm

Plate 12

The reverse of plate 11.

Chinese bell flowers on the front. The reverse is painted with three heart-shaped peaches, leaves and distinctive spirals, all connected with loosely drawn tendrils. In addition there is a pair of concentric rings finely drawn around the foot rim and a further single ring between these and the painting of the tendrils. The autumnal plants are drawn in outline with a sharp blue line and the leaves and petals are carefully shaded with a wash to achieve the desired effect. Arita decorators used precisely this technique in the 18th century in the production of their finest wares for the home market. The centre of each of the bases is inscribed, "Dedicated on behalf of Hirado Matsura Lord of Hizen Province by Makiyama Enrin of Tamaokiyama in the eighth, hare, year of Kyoho". Kyoho 8 is equivalent to 1723 in the Western calendar. Careful study of these dishes shows that the clay is extremely fine, of a pure white hue with none of the grittiness often found in Arita wares. The glaze is thick, even over the flat areas of the dish, only pooling at either side of the foot rim, and possesses a soft quality that is entirely different to the harsher, glossier glazes of other kilns. It also has a definite greenish tint which is particularly noticeable where it pools. The dishes are thinly potted and the slight waviness of the outside rim is deliberately shaped to achieve a soft and gentle effect. Overall they are of a high quality with few kiln flaws, the product of a proficient and experienced kiln that was clearly able to make wares to a high standard. The painting itself is delicate, demonstrating a certain freedom of brushstroke that is clearly visible despite the fact that there are five dishes of the same pattern. There is significantly less spontaneity and freedom in the painting of another set of bowls and covers[1] painted with floating blossom and dated 1759.

Having established a type of porcelain and decoration known to have been made in 1723, it is reasonable to assume that pieces of the same type were made at about that time. Small food dishes, generally in sets of five or multiples thereof, were being made in large quantities by the Arita kilns during this period and the general similarities between these and Arita examples are obvious. The major differences are the painting on

[1]   Ill. *Noda II, pl* 333

the reverse, the purity of the paste and the colour and texture of the glaze. This inscription by the Matsura lord establishes them as Hirado ware. Dishes of similar size displaying the aforementioned qualities of glaze and body are to be found painted with landscapes (plates 13 & 14), vines, pine, other

Plate 13

A dish painted with a rocky outcrop beside a lake, the reverse with scrolling branches of peaches and curled tendrils. Somewhat lighter in colour than the octagonal bottles and the painting showing less spontaneity, the paste and glaze of this piece are very close to that of the dish dated 1723 and made at a similar time. Diameter 14.0 cm

Plate 14
The reverse of plate 13. The similarity to the dish dated 1723 (plates 8 and 9) is clearly illustrated, this example having slightly more colour in the glaze. The unusual execution of the oval scrolling tendrils is a distinctive feature of early 18th century Hirado.

varieties of flower and the crests of the Matsura family. As a group they demonstrate a significant difference in artistic characteristics to comparable products of the Arita or Kakiemon kilns.

Items that predate this group are likely to be less technically perfect though still made from a fine white body, as we know the clay that would allow this to be made was found in 1662. Thematically akin to the dish illustrated in plate 13, is a small group of less than ten faceted bottles (plates 10, 15 & 16) now spread in collections worldwide. They are all made from a very white clay that is not at all granular and the glaze has a strong greenish or greenish-yellow tint. In this respect they are similar to the set of dishes dated 1723 and appear to be made from the same materials. In other respects they differ. The technical quality is inferior to the dishes. The glaze is unevenly applied, often pooling to one side or another to create a discoloured area. More often than not they have warped in the kiln and no longer sit perfectly upright. Brownish dust particles present during firing have settled on the horizontal surfaces showing they were not efficiently protected in the kiln. In construction, these bottles were moulded in two halves and joined together. The vertical line showing the join is often still visible (plate 17) and has not been fully removed by smoothing as would have been expected in the finely finished wares of the 18th century.

They are not the products of a kiln that was able to produce wares as fine as the 1723 dishes. The attention to detail is lacking and had they emerged from the kiln at that date they would have been discarded as rejects. Technically the potting is far inferior to fine quality Arita wares of the early 18th century. On technical grounds alone, there is a very strong case to suggest these bottles date from the late 17th century as the quality of these bottles is similar to most pieces produced in the Arita kilns at that time. It is unlikely that the Hirado potters would have begun to gain their reputation for fine wares had they been making objects that were significantly inferior to those of their

Plate 15

The base of the octagonal bottle shown in plate 10. The pooling of the glaze causing a yellowish hue particularly to the left side is clearly visible, as is the unequal size of the facets. Also discernible are the reddish orange patches on parts of the unglazed footring caused by the oxidation of iron impurities in the clay that emerge along the unprotected edge of the glaze during firing. This is often a sign of Hirado origin.

Plate 16
Detail of a 17th century octagonal bottle. Compare with plate 10. The paintings are essentially a mirror image of each other, yet in every individual detail they differ indicating they were probably painted by an artist rather than a trained ceramic decorator.

Plate 17

An octagonal bottle[2], typical of the late 17th century, this example differs from those previously recorded in that it is painted with boys at play under a pine tree rather than a rugged landscape. It is possible that this was painted by Katayama Shoshun, the reputed inventor of the famous pattern and court artist to the Matsura.
Height 19.0 cm

rivals and immediate neighbours. Neither would Matsura Chinshin have dared to present pieces from his kilns to the Emperor's court in 1700 had they not made a very favourable comparison. The proximity of Arita means that there must have been an exchange of information between the local kilns and that there could not have been any significant difference in technical quality for more than a few years if Hirado was to become a ceramic of respected quality and bear favourable comparison at the courts of mainland Japan.

2   *Illustrated pl 100b in Jenyns and formerly in Jenyns' collection*

Of the known examples of the group of faceted bottles, all but one are decorated with landscapes and essentially picture the same rugged hills and pavilions. Had this scene been painted in this manner on a scroll or screen, there is no doubt that the consensus of opinion would date it between the early 17th and early 18th century. Painting from an earlier date would probably have been less congested, while later painting would have included yet more elements and certainly have lacked the freshness of these examples. The painting of these bottles is spirited, demonstrating the qualities of an artist as opposed to a trained ceramic decorator. Each bottle has essentially the same pattern, sometimes in mirror image, yet different in detail so, that some are more artistically successful than others. The strength of colour and differing juxtaposition of the elements on the scenes produce a variety of effects, as though the painter was creating a new version of the same scene on each bottle. We can establish a date ranging between 1662 and 1723 at the extremes and a late 17th century year of manufacture is most likely. As we have seen,

records show that court artists were involved in the efforts of the
kilns at Mikawachi and it is therefore likely that Katayama
Shokei, or his brother Shoshun painted these bottles.

The odd one out in this group of eight-sided sake
bottles is painted with a scene of boys chasing butterflies under a
pine tree (plate 17). Displaying rather fewer technical flaws, it is
clearly of a similar or slightly later date. The design derives from
Ming blue and white porcelain, where the theme of boys playing
was commonly found, but it is reputed that Katayama Shoshun
was the first to "reinvent" the design and apply it to porcelain.
It has since become the most popular of Hirado patterns,
surviving until the demise of the kilns and is almost regarded as
the trade mark of Hirado wares. There is a legend that persists to
this day that claims that pieces painted with seven boys are of the
highest quality, those with five of a slightly lower standard and
those with only three more mundane. Although the story could be
based in truth, it is evident that soon after the start of production
this tenet was disregarded. There are some exceptionally fine
pieces with five and even three boys while not all examples with a
greater number of boys are superior. Certainly in later years it
seems that the number of boys used in the design was a function

Plate 19

*The base of an 18th century cup
stand showing the dense white
hue of the paste and neat, even
rings either side of the foot ring.
The reddish orange colouration
caused by the emergence of iron
oxide during firing at the edge of
the glaze is clearly visible.*

Plate 20

An ogee form brush washer with everted lip painted with a continuous scene of pavilions in a rugged mountainous landscape. The painterly quality of the decoration is close to the late 17th century faceted bottles and indicates that it predates the more carefully composed decoration of late 18th century pieces. Diameter 7.0 cm

Plate 21

A square water dropper on four feet modelled in low relief with cranes among clouds. This is typical of the fine quality yet utilitarian products that the Hirado kilns made for the Matsura family in the 19th century. 6.9 cm square

of the shape of the piece rather than any attempt to define quality by a predetermined number of children.

Of the other forms which seem to date from this era, there are several examples of small cup stands painted with landscapes, an interesting sake bottle of brick form painted with boys playing on a bridge on some facets and flowers on others. There are also plates painted with flowers and tendrils, and bowls, some with Matsura crests and others with landscapes. An interesting example of early Mikawachi ware is in plate 22, a fan-form incense dish painted with a free-spirited rendition of a flowering prunus. The short curved edge remains unglazed, showing it was held during firing by a shaped support and sat vertically in the kiln. This indicates a lack of experience in firing, particularly as the dish has three small feet on the reverse which would have provided ample support and would not have left so visible an unglazed area. The kiln flaws are severe enough for it to have been discarded in a later era. The painting is not that of a decorator copying a pattern but of an artist quickly sketching a prunus to capture the hardy and spiky characteristics of the plant.

Pear shaped bottles with bold floral, animal or bird decoration are a well known type of Hirado ware (plate 6) that were made for the domestic market. Generally painted with bold brushstrokes in strong darkish blue, often beneath lappet borders, they were also in production at Arita from the 1670–80's. Plate 23 shows a bottle that belongs to this group. The softness and delicacy of colour differs from typical Arita bottles and the method of painting, particularly of the pine trees and the pavilions, and attention to the effects of deliberately soft shading are more akin to Hirado than Arita. Landscapes on Arita porcelains are less common than floral or bird-decorated wares and those that exist show little of the intricacy and complexity displayed on the continuous scene around this bottle. The paste itself is whiter and finer than that normally associated with Arita wares of this period. The piece thus demonstrates many of the features the Hirado painters were trying to achieve, including a

Plate 22
*A fan form incense dish painted
with a spiky prunus blossom.
The spontaneous quality of the
painting in Kano style, the
numerous kiln flaws, the scale of
the object, the colour of the glaze
and its soft texture all indicate a
very early date for this small dish.
Diameter 13.5 cm*

subtler, softer feel than the Arita wares and would suggest that this high quality piece was an attempt to imitate the wares of Hirado that were fast gaining an enviable reputation for exceptional quality.

There are also examples of ceramics currently attributed to Arita that in fact may have their origins in Hirado. An example of this may be the sculpted white models of hawks on brown glazed rock work bases often attributed to Arita. Another could be the pair of ormolu mounted vases in the form of cycad trees belonging to Her Majesty the Queen and exhibited at the British Museum in its exhibition in 1990 "Porcelain for Palaces"[3]. There are no parallels to these in known Arita types and they display typical Hirado colouration, modelling, glaze and paste colour. Above all they display an eccentricity of concept that is typically Hirado. Interestingly, there are also unmounted examples of almost identical vases in Hirado Castle and other museums on Hirado Island. There can be little doubt that these are products from the Hirado kilns though they may not date back

3   *Illustrated p.115, no.71*

quite as far as the 17th century; the European bronze mounts are in the manner of Duplessis and could have been made soon after the porcelain arrived in Europe. Jean-Claude Duplessis (died 1774) was born in Turin and is best known for his work as a designer and modeller for the Sevres factory. He seems to have also worked extensively for the marchands mercier as a sculptor of decorative bronzes but there is very little documented work by him. Known to have made the mounts for the Bureau du Roi Louis XV at Versailles and also for a Sevres vase given by the Dauphine, Marie-Joseph de Saxe, to her father Augustus III,

Plate 23

A large pear shaped vase painted with a landscape beneath lappets, feather and ruyi forms. The distinctly soft tone of blue, expertly controlled suggests this is an attempt by the late 17th century Arita decorator to work in Hirado manner. Though fine, the paste is distinctly Arita, displaying a granular rather than dense texture. Height 37 cm

King of Saxony, in 1749, these fine gilt bronze mounts are almost certainly by Duplessis and from the mid 18th century. The date of the porcelain must be prior to this.

Pieces decorated with landscapes that relate to the group of early faceted bottles include the rectangular box[4] (App.6, no.68) in the Guimet Museum in Paris painted with a typical Hirado landscape around the sides and the five lobed mulberry leaf crest of the Hirado daimyo centrally on the top. The base is flat and unglazed. The painting of the landscape is closely allied to that of the faceted bottles but is beginning to show more deliberate care in its execution. By no means technically perfect, its heavy warped body has the imperfections found on the faceted bottles and it is likely to date from the late 17th century or the first years of the 18th century. Another landscape example is the thickly potted globular tripod koro[5] with handles (plate 24) to be found in the important collection of Oriental porcelain in the Dresden Porcelain Collection, Germany. Originally from one of the many other Saxon palaces outside Dresden, it was subsequently brought into the collection and its inventory mark suggests an 18th century acquisition. This is not conclusive of an early date in the century as the Saxon electors did not employ the same system of inventory marking as the primary Dresden collection.

In making a comparison between the 17th century painting of these landscapes and 18th century examples, one can see an increasingly studied care in the painting that evolved into the meticulous and highly detailed painting on the straight sided water jar (plate 25) dated 1835, and later deteriorated in an overelaborate and repetitive style.

All the porcelain made at Mikawachi at this time, and indeed until about 1800, was for the use of the Matsura family, either for gifts to present to others, for their personal needs or for use by their court and retainers. These early wares always have a practical purpose in a Japanese household and include such forms as water jars (plates 26 & 27), flower vases, tea caddies,

4 G 4976 *Grandidier Collection acquired prior to 1908*

5 P.O. 2542/1361

Plate 24

A *tripod koro painted with landscape beneath a formal scrolling border. Thickly potted and heavy, this koro is typical of early 18th century Hirado. The base with 18th century Saxon palace inventory mark.*
(App.6, no.71)
Height 15.0 cm

sake cups and bottles (plates 10 & 17), tea cups (for green tea), tea bowls (for the tea ceremony), food bowls and covers, cup stands, incense burners (plates 24 & 28), incense boxes, small food dishes (plates 11 & 13) and sauce ewers. At the same time, models were added to the wide range of items and included netsuke, okimono (plates 29, 30 & 31), water droppers and weights (plates 32 & 33). All of these are small pieces; large items over 25 cms were scarcely made in the 18th century.

Initially the range of decorative themes on 18th century wares is comparatively limited and it is not until later that the variety of subject matter expands to attain the diversity for which Hirado has become renowned. Landscapes, used in the 17th century, maintained their popularity throughout the kiln's lifetime, as did the pattern of boys chasing butterflies under a pine tree. Other subjects that were used in the 18th century include a variety of flowers, vines and other plants with trailing tendrils,

Plate 25

A straight sided water jar meticulously painted with pavilions in an elaborate landscape. This piece elaborately inscribed and dated 1835 (App.6, no.86) helps in establishing the style of decoration, type of paste and glaze used at Mikawachi at this point in their history. Height 18.0 cm

Plate 26

Among the most successful artistic achievements of the Hirado potters and painters, this water jar[6] combines superb painting with exquisite modelling. The 18th century landscape painting with the rabbit finial and mask handles help to establish that three dimensional work was being made at this time. Height 21.6 cm

6   Formerly in the collection of the late John Popr

58

Plate 27

A water jar and cover painted with a dragon emerging from waves between jewelled archaic dragon borders. The form and decoration of this water jar is very close to others illustrated in Brinkley and the catalogue of the sale of pieces from the Matsura family collection in 1928.
18th century. Height 19.05 cm

dragons and phoenix. Human figure painting was introduced, the commonest being in those in Chinese dress (plates 17 & 34) and the rarest in Japanese costume (plate 35). While decoration may have often been based on Chinese originals, the shapes of the pieces are quintessentially Japanese and can often be seen in the products of other Japanese kilns, such as the shaped bowls and other small table wares made in Arita, particularly by Kakiemon.

Since Matsura Chinshin established his tea ceremony school, there had always been a need for utensils that could be used at such occasions and the Mikawachi kilns made many such articles. They made a greater proportion of pieces for tea ceremony use than any other porcelain kiln. Porcelain water jars that originate from Arita are rarely found but examples from Hirado are relatively common. These were first made from the

Plate 28
A koro and pierced cover, the finial formed as a finely sculpted deer, painted with branches of maple. This small incense burner exemplifies the finest Hirado wares of the earlier 18th century.
Height 8.25 cm

Plate 29
A white okimono of a mythical baku. Identical to another example datable to 1801, this heavy, almost solid model shows that production of three dimensional sculpture at the Hirado kiln was in full flow by the end of the 18th century.
Length 15 cm

60

Plate 30

A miniature model of a seated sage holding a fan. Although moulded in many individual parts, this okimono has been hand finished in every detail. The solid construction, density and weight indicate an early date, possibly 18th century. Length 10.5 cm

Plate 31

A model of a boar sleeping in the shade of a chrysanthemum beside a rock, coloured in blue, brown and grey. Typical of pieces and often thought to date from the last years of the 19th century, this extraordinary model was created at least 80 years prior. Length 12.6 cm

61

Plate 32
Important in establishing that fine sculptural work was made long before the Meiji era, this fine chestnut branch is part of the treasures acquired by von Siebold prior to 1828. Length 16.0 cm

Plate 33
A selection of weights formed as flowers. These flowers were made from the late 18th century though most date from the early part of the 19th. Unbelievably fragile, it is astonishing that any have survived though there are several examples in museums that are entirely undamaged. This group uses celadon as well as the more usual blue and brown. They were fired lying flat in the kiln and consequently the underneath is generally sculpted but left unglazed. Length of largest 12.5 cm

Plate 34

A bulbous tea pot and cover with moulded bamboo handle painted with Chinese sages at leisure, the lid with books, brushes and musical instruments; the unglazed base signed. (App.6, no.27) Height 19.5 cm

Plate 35 & 36

A cylindrical koro on three feet painted with attendants leading a general on his horse to water, the reverse with flower sprays emerging from rock work. This is a typical early 18th century incense burner (koro), similar to those well-represented in the Walters Art Gallery and bears all the distinctive elements of early Hirado wares such as a soft glaze with a hint of greenish blue colour as well as the gentle blue colouration that the painters were trying to achieve. Diameter 7.6 cm

Plate 37

A globular water jar and cover painted with a single scene of a mounted samurai and his retainers above stylised chrysanthemum in waves, the lid with tiger finial. Late Edo period. Height 23.0 cm

18th century and although the form and style of decoration evolved and changed, they continued to be produced until the kiln closed. It was these water jars produced in the second half of the 18th century that first introduced three dimensional modelling for the lids were sometimes surmounted with a knob in the shape of humans or animals (plate 37). The Amakusa clay was ideally suited for these small sculptures, because after firing, it still showed the sharp lines the potter had imparted to the model, even when covered in a relatively thick glaze.

A comparison between Arita and Hirado models shows that fine sculptural details remain intact on Hirado examples, whereas they disappear or become hazy on Arita pieces. The development of these finials into three dimensional objects that stand alone is discussed in chapter five.

19th century Hirado

Among the most interesting Hirado porcelain collections in Western museums that of the Metropolitan Museum of Art in New York. One aspect of its importance lies in the fact that, apart from a small handful of pieces it was assembled prior to 1893 by Captain F. Brinkley, the renowned English orientalist who lived in Japan for many years and wrote extensively on a wide variety of aspects of Japanese and Chinese culture and history. His major work was published in 1901 and comprises eight volumes entitled "Japan, its history, arts and literature", followed by a further four on the same aspects of China. Volume eight titled "Keramic Art" is a detailed and comprehensive study of the history of the ceramic industry of Japan. Brinkley's understanding of Japanese ceramics is clearly displayed in this book and his enthusiasm for the wares made at Mikawachi abounds. He writes in great detail, listing members of the families of potters who worked for the Matsura daimyo, but even more interestingly he extols the virtues, both technical and artistic, of the wares themselves. The extent of his collection of porcelain as a whole is not known but the Metropolitan houses 111 pieces.

Captain Brinkley sold part of his collection of Hirado to the wealthy American, Charles Stewart Smith, in 1892 while he and his new bride were honeymooning in Japan. The following year Smith donated the 69 Hirado pieces he had just acquired to The Metropolitan Museum. A year later Captain Brinkley sold another group of 42 Hirado pieces to Mrs. V. Everit Macy, who also left these to the same museum at her death in 1923. Thus two significant groups of Captain Brinkley's collection were reunited. A study of the collection reveals a sophisticated understanding of the subject and an appreciation for the outstanding quality of Hirado. An early collection such as this demonstrates that, contrary to more recent supposition, the products from Mikawachi were made for use in Japan, as not one of the 111 pieces was made for export. Although one must remember that these pieces were selected by one man's taste and are not necessarily representative of the products of the kiln as a whole, it is interesting to study them as a group because they

Brinkley and Walters: early Western enthusiasts.

give us an overview of 18th century output. Captain Brinkley chose only pieces of the finest quality; the consistently high level of potting and painting is immediately evident. The majority of the pieces date from the 18th century. Apart from the fine selection of small figures, the forms are generally simple. The decoration of each of these 18th century pieces is classically Edo in taste, with many designs derived from Ming and Ching blue and white wares. Straight-sided water jars with formal scrolling patterns[1] or dragons chasing the flaming pearl[2] are taken almost directly from 15th century originals, while others formed as sections of bamboo painted with sages in a bamboo grove[3] derive from even earlier Chinese ceramic decoration. A water jar painted with a dragon is illustrated in plate 27. Interestingly it is of the same form and pattern, (except that a kirin replaces the dragon as the central motif), as another illustrated in Brinkley's own book. A third water jar pictured in the catalogue of the sale of the Matsura family collection at The Tokyo Bijitsu Club in 1928 as lot 457, fetched 369 Yen, a sum that would have been enough to buy a house in those times! The strong Chinese influence on Hirado porcelains of the 18th century is evident in this collection and although the purity of the designs and forms diminished in later years, this inspiration remained prevalent throughout the kiln's existence.

The group of four small koro in the Metropolitan Museum's collection, all products of the 18th century, illustrate some of the other styles made at Mikawachi at this time. The straight-sided koro painted with boys romping and chasing butterflies[4] derives from Chinese Ming porcelain. The design of the lid, which is finely pierced with a naturalistic pattern of leaves and flowers, is entirely Japanese in origin, as is the decoration of the cylindrical koro on three feet painted with sparse sprays of flowers against a fence[5] and also the globular koro painted with a maple[6], whose lid is surmounted by a fine model of a deer (plate 28). A fourth incense burner[7] is illustrated in Captain Brinkley's book and is uniquely Japanese. The central cylindrical column is painted with sprays of leaves and the whole is encased in a fine lattice work of crisscrossed porcelain almost in imitation

[1]   23.225.111, 93.3.40, & 93.3.273

[2]   93.3.3, 93.3.4

[3]   23.225.53, 23.225.54, 23.225.63 & 23.225.74

[4]   93.3.293

[5]   23.225.95

[6]   93.3.11

[7]   93.3.5

Plate 39

*A bottle vase with slender neck painted with geese
among reeds beneath ruyi and lappet borders;
the base signed. (App.6, no.28) The light weight
of this fine vase indicates a Meiji rather than
earlier date. Height 26.4 cm*

Plate 40

A two handled chocolate cup and
saucer painted with carp, marked
on the base in underglaze blue
with the European letters
"H.K(?)". (App.6, no.70)
The initials on the base suggest
that this was part of a special
order for export; the European
form lends support to this theory.
Diameter of saucer 14.0 cm

69

Plate 41

A bowl with barbed and everted rim decorated with shaped floral panels in Chinese 17th century Kraak style. This piece is a 19th century Japanese example. Had it not been marked "Hirado san", (App.6, no.17) together with the painters' name, it could not necessarily have been identified as a product of the Mikawachi kilns. Diameter 19.9 cm

Plate 42

An oviform sake pot, the handle and spout formed as a dragon, painted with cocks and hens. The lid, with extended plug, surmounted by a finely modelled cock. The sophisticated technique and the intense whiteness of the body displayed in the manufacture of this ewer suggest an early Meiji date. This is supported by the use of unrelated motifs on the same piece—a phenomenon not usually associated with the Edo period. Height 23.2 cm

of basket weave. This extraordinary type of reticulation, evident here and in the lid of the koro first mentioned, became a hallmark of Hirado wares. It was used from the 18th century, though the majority of such pieces date from late in the following century when forms became more complex and overall design less simple.

Another important collector active in the 19th century was William Walters of Baltimore. A wealthy industrialist who made his fortune from the railways, he began collecting a wide range of art works in the mid 1850's and was one of the first Americans to build a collection of Oriental ceramics. A significant number of pieces was added to the already large collection at the centennial exhibition in Philadelphia in 1876, where Walters bought a great deal of Oriental porcelain including several antique and new pieces from the Hirado kilns. Like that at the Metropolitan Museum, the collection comprises many pieces from the 18th century but also includes examples that date through the late Edo and Meiji periods. After the significant acquisitions of 1876, further pieces were added to the holdings and, subsequent to his death in 1894, by his son Henry Walters. The entire collection of both European and Oriental art, including the 99 pieces of Hirado porcelain, is now housed in The Walters Art Gallery in Baltimore and unlike many museum collections, a significant number of their important Hirado holdings are on permanent view. Possibly the earliest piece in the Walters collection is a food bowl and cover decorated with both of the two different Matsura family mon and bordered with formal foliate scrolls[8]. It is large, thickly potted and extremely heavy; a late 17th or early 18th century date is likely[9]. The collection houses an astonishingly large group of nineteen small 18th century koros of cylindrical or globular form, some with reticulated porcelain covers, painted with the full range of subject matters used on such pieces. It is not only these early examples of Hirado that are so interesting, but also the extension of the collection from this period through the 19th century. There are many fine examples of early and mid 19th century wares but

[8]   49.1538

[9]   *Compare with bowl illustrated in Noda II no.95, dated to the 17th century*

Plate 43

A slender meiping form vase decorated with scattered Togugawa mon on an incised ground, the shoulder and base with lappets. As this was made as a gift for the shogun it clearly dates from the Edo era. Whether it was made in 18th or 19th century is an interesting issue that is open to debate.
Height 18.5 cm

unfortunately not much significant documentary material to aid in the establishment of specific dates for particular Hirado types, although many were acquired by known dates in the 19th century. There are some exceptions and it may be that further reconciliation of the extant documentation will help in the future. Interestingly, the museum's records show that the pure white water jar[10] with low relief decoration of solitary flower sprays was purchased at the Paris exhibition of 1878.

It is, however, the first half of the 19th century that provides the greatest number of Hirado pieces marked with dates (see appendix 3 for a complete list). We have already seen the

10 49.1734

Plate 44

*An elaborate lantern or incense burner
with reticulated hinged door entwined by
dragons and painted with four landscape
scenes on the stepped base, cranes to the
upper part. These imposing and intricate
pieces are likely to have been made for
export, possibly to China, as their
aesthetic is far removed from that of
Edo wares but is paralleled by other
early Meiji export ceramics and
metalwork. Height 49.4 cm*

Plate 45

*Snow covered huts beneath a giant pine.
Detail from one side of the base of plate 44.*

Plate 46
A large plate decorated in blue and low relief with crabs at the water's edge. Sea creatures of almost every kind were a popular subject throughout Hirado's production. This unusually large dish is an example of the best of the kiln's work from Meiji times combining both delicate painting as well as fine low relief work. Diameter 38.1 cm

Plate 47
A *globular bottle vase*[11] *with elongated neck decorated in low relief with ho-o birds flying among peony painted in blue. The purity of form, the interplay between the two methods of decoration and the quality of its execution make this one of Hirado's 19th century masterpieces. Height 28.2 cm*

11   *Formerly in the collection of Richard de la Mare and illustrated in Garner*

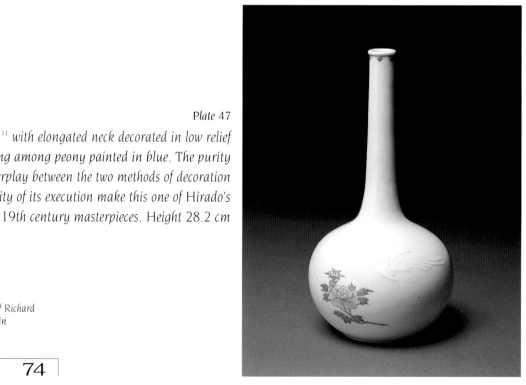

water jar with landscape dated 1835, and there are further examples within a year of this date that give a clear picture of the type of material made, the subject matter used in decoration and the technical quality of potting, glazing and finishing extant at this time. Flowers and vines, landscapes, tortoises and of course versions of the now renowned pattern of boys chasing butterflies under a pine tree, all painted on pieces of essentially simple shape, are typical.

In addition to these dated examples there is a further relevant source of information that is briefly mentioned here, though other aspects will be discussed in chapter 5. Much of the collection now housed in the National Museum of Ethnology, Leiden, Holland was assembled prior to 1828. Collected by the multi-talented Dr. Philipp Franz Balthasar von Siebold (1796–1862), the main importance of its vast array of ethnographica lies in areas other than ceramics. Among its 7,000 items however is a small but significant group of over 30 Hirado pieces ascribed to the Mikawachi kilns that were known to exist before 1828 when they were removed from Japan. They conform to the decorative themes shown in the two important collections in the Metropolitan Museum and the Walters Gallery.

The understated decoration, modest size and plain traditional forms in these three groups all suggest that the flamboyant era of Hirado was yet to come. The Leiden collection gives us proof that low relief decoration was being used on Hirado by this date; it can be seen, used in a simple and uncomplicated way, on an incense burner[12] and a food warmer[13], hinting at the more elaborate low relief work that was to come in later years. A second fact that can be deduced from the wares at Leiden is the existence of the unique and spectacular models of flowers at this early date. These will be discussed in chapter 5.

There is thus a clear picture emerging of the type of pieces produced at the kilns at Mikawachi at this time. They are

[12] 1-1804
[13] 1-493

small pieces for use by the Matsura family and their entourage. It is evident that porcelain was made for all ranks in the Matsura establishment. In addition the wide divergence in quality, both of painting and potting, further this argument as it would be most unlikely that the poorer quality items would have been intended for use by the senior ranks of the Matsura hierarchy.

In 1828 an event entirely beyond the control of the Mikawachi artisans changed the style of their products and introduced new and exciting aspects to their work. In this year, a typhoon devastated the Arita potteries. Although located very close by, the winds failed to inflict any severe damage on the kilns at Mikawachi. This tragedy reduced the production of the Arita kilns to a trickle until they were able to rebuild and left an opportunity for other rivals to fill the demand for export wares. To fill this void the Hirado Trading Company was established at Mikawachi in 1830. To establish a clear picture of the scale of operation at Mikawachi, it is interesting to note that there were 18 official potters, 51 assistants and six decorators among over 300 individuals working at the kilns at any given time between 1830 and 1847.

Plates 48–51

Paintings of Hirado and its environs executed in 1842 by Katayama Shoei.

14 *Illustrated Cardeiro no.7, p.48*

Plate 52

A finely potted eggshell beaker decorated in overglaze enamels with musicians. Large quantities of finely potted eggshell tableware destined for Western households were made at Mikawachi and then overdecorated, often to a high technical standard in outside workshops. This example was enamelled by Hichozan Shimpo whose mark can be found on the base. Meiji period.
Diameter 9.1 cm

We can get a picture of Hirado at this time because of a pair of long scrolls (plates 48–51) comprising over 12 individual paintings of Hirado, including the castle, the bay, Kurokoshima Island and street scenes painted in 1842 by Katayama Shoei, whose art name was Suiunsai, show the location as it was at the time. Comparisons with the painting on the porcelain are interesting, particularly the distinctive sails on the fishing boats so often seen in the landscape paintings, the snow covered trees and the familiar variations of conifers.

There had already been a limited amount of trade with the Dutch in the very first years of the century which had ceased during the latter years of the Napoleonic wars in Europe and it was this trade that they looked to increase. They made very fine white eggshell porcelain that was a development from the sets of fine bowls and covers created during the 18th century and was suitable for European style tea sets. Those known to have been among the potters making such wares include Ikeda Anjiro, Takahashi Heisuke, Nakazato Santaro and Furukawa Shosaku.

Another departure from the former everyday wares fulfilled a
demand for brightly coloured overglaze enamel decoration
(plate 52). Although a majority of enamelled pieces were
decorated outside Mikawachi, some of this work was also carried
out at the kilns. Hirado enamelled wares are discussed in more
detail in chapter six.

It was during this period that the Matsura family
gradually began to reduce its direct patronage of the kilns. The
fortunes of the clan had begun to decline from the extraordinarily
powerful and wealthy position they had held at the pinnacle of
their achievement in the 16th and 17th centuries. Their major
source of income, trade, had been whittled away until it was
finally removed by the relocation of the Dutch trading post to
Nagasaki. Subsequently, though remaining extremely wealthy,
they were unable to replace this loss and depended on capital
acquired earlier, as well as their stipend from the shogun. By the
early 19th century, the Matsura no longer saw the need for the
luxury of their own exclusive kiln and decided to reduce their
economic support for the venture. The formation of a new
organisation to make porcelain for export must have eased their
financial burdens, but they formally withdrew their patronage in
1843. That is not to say that they no longer had any association
with the creation of Hirado porcelain, as an article in the
Manchester Guardian of 1891 indicates. It gives an excellent
descriptive picture of a potter working on a special commission at
the magnificent Matsura palace in Tokyo, demonstrating the close
involvement of the family, and its continuing interest in ceramics
and their personal involvement in its production.

But from 1843 onwards, all the products of the kiln
were available to those wishing to buy them and the kiln was no
longer an exclusive enclave of the Matsura. The result was a
gradual change in the style of wares produced at the kiln. No
longer was the norm the conservative form and decoration often
derived from or inspired by Chinese porcelain; rather in the
ensuing years, the wares reflected the public demand for more

elaborate shapes and embellishment that culminated in the production of wares that combined the influences of several different artistic schools.

Unique to the Mikawachi kilns are porcelain flower vases of a form unlike anything made at any other kiln. Originating in the last years of the 18th century, their development received a major impetus in the 1830's, parallel with the expansion and changes within the kilns themselves. The basic form, a bulbous body with exaggerated flaring of the neck, is derived from bronze flower vases, themselves conceived in the 17th century to accommodate large formal flower arrangements that played a part in secular and religious ceremonies. Vases of this form generally have applied handles (plates 55 & 56), mostly shaped as animals or as animal heads again inspired by bronze vases (plate 54). Yet others have a vertical rim applied to the top edge (plate 55). Other embellishments include the use of carving or moulded low relief work. At their best, these vases of strong and powerful form combined with high quality painting or low relief sculpture, are some of the most successful artistic achievements of the Edo period in porcelain. When the painters or potters over elaborate, it is my view that their artistic impact is diminished. Examples of this form are however rare (particularly in undamaged condition) and rank among the most distinctive and important works of the Mikawachi kilns. Interestingly, no other kiln made vases of this shape and the most likely reason for this is the inability of clay other than that from Amakusa, to sustain this demanding form during manufacture.

Another small but highly significant group of Hirado porcelain are those referred to by David Hyatt King as "presentation pieces"[15]. I can find no reason to refer to them as such, but stylistically they form an extraordinary group of elaborate porcelains of large size, often with high relief dragons, incised low relief patterns or openwork reticulation. The painting is usually of the highest quality, as is the exceptional modelling of any finials or applied three dimensional sculptural work. It is

[15] TOCS 1980–1, *pp.*20–22

Plate 53

A bulbous vase with exaggerated flaring rim painted with a frolicking shishi. This form is derived from bronze flower vases. The earliest examples date from the turn of the 18th century, though others, like this, date from the late Meiji period. Height 36.2 cm

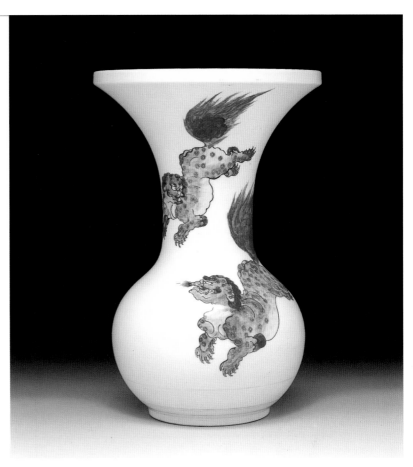

Plate 54

A bulbous bronze flower vase with flaring rim and butterfly handles. Bronzes of this exaggerated form were used in Japan at least from the early 18th century and it appears that the Hirado potters were influenced by this when creating vases of similar shape. Height 27.3 cm

Plate 55

A baluster vase with flaring rim and applied frog handles painted with geese among reeds beneath a a brocade border. The technical difficulties in firing this top heavy shape was a constant battle for the Hirado potters even at the end of the Edo period. Nevertheless the distortion to the rim does little to diminish the appeal of this piece. Height 34.0 cm

my belief that these form the core of a larger group of pieces that are of the same quality but perhaps not as spectacular in concept or size as this elite selection. Hyatt King, in his paper in "The Transactions of The Oriental Ceramic Society" (1980/81) suggests a date of 1820–30 for the earliest of these, with most of them being made prior to 1870. I can find only the most tenuous evidence to support this and would suggest that in fact they evolved later in the 19th century from globular water jars with elaborate finials. Initially forms remained simple but were embellished with both incised and applied low relief work. The painting is of the finest quality though the effect of a slightly hazy underglaze blue so typical of Hirado wares is sometimes found on these pieces. The form became more elaborate as time went on and sometimes pieces from this group were applied with high relief decoration, most commonly dragons.

During the Meiji era the painted decoration often encompassed more than one theme. Representative of this is the lidded jar (plate 57) with its integrated base, applied decoration of a male and female dragon wrapped round the body of the vase, the shishi finial and the flying crane decoration above the finely painted lappet border. Essentially the form was based on a form of lidded jar commonly produced at Arita in the late 17th and

Plate 56
A bulbous vase with exaggerated flaring rim and applied frog handles painted with weeping willow over water. The theme of this vase refers to the legend of Ono no Tofu, a celebrated Chinese calligrapher and minister who tried seven times to gain a higher governmental post without success. Sitting at the side of a lake bemoaning his lot he noticed a frog attempting to spring from the lake to the willow. Having failed in many attempts, the frog finally succeeded. This led Ono no Tofu to persist in his attempts to further his career and he rose to become first minister. Late Edo period. Height 32.5 cm

early 18th century. It is unlikely that the diversity of themes employed on these Hirado versions would have occurred in the Edo period and it is my opinion that such pieces are products typical of Meiji times. William Walters had acquired a now famous example, now in his Gallery, by 1893. Many of the larger pieces in the group are marked with characters reading "Dai Nihon, Hirado san," sometimes with the addition of the artist's name. The inclusion of the words "Dai Nihon" (Great Japan) on works of art in porcelain or other media is generally accepted as a Meiji phenomenon, seldom used earlier, and is reflective of the strong nationalistic mood in the country at this time.

As to the artistic style itself, they do not sit comfortably with other art works of Edo times and one must question their practical purpose if they were made at this early date. I refer to

Plate 57

Often referred to as "a presentation piece" this elaborate jar and cover with integral stand is decorated with applied dragons and painted with cranes above lappets and wave patterns, the finial formed as a shishi. The assemblage of unrelated motifs suggest a Meiji date for this impressive vase rather than earlier when such combinations of design had yet to become popular. (App.6, no.48) Height 37.3 cm

Plate 58
*This set of three, probably
intended for the altar is an
astonishing tour de force in
the art of reticulation.
It is typical of the high
quality work of the Meiji
era. Signed differently on
the base of each vase.
(App.6, nos.10 & 11)
Height of koro 38.1 cm*

Hyatt King's own excellent description of them when he states
that they "combine a detailed naturalism, whose origin is
contemporary Europe, with the Japanese tradition of ceramic
sculpture. They recreate the Sino-Japanese bronze models in
porcelain. Overall, the effect is high Victorian and worthy of
Burges or Garnier." [i.e. archetypal Victoriana of the latter part of
the 19th century and therefore Meiji rather than Edo]. Other
Japanese works of art that similarly combine elements of
decoration from diverse sources put together in elaborate style
(such as Satsuma earthenware or bronzes) are datable to the first
part of the Meiji era when outside influences prompted a
regression from the usual sensibilities of balance and form
associated with Japanese design. While it is most likely that such
pieces were made for export to the West to satisfy the taste of the
very wealthy (for indeed only the wealthy could have afforded
these expensive and extraordinary high quality pieces that are a
tour-de-force of the ceramicist's art) there is an alternative
possibility. It could be that they were made for export to China.

The elaborate dragons clambering round the pieces are typical of Empress Tzu Hsi's flamboyant taste and they would be entirely at home in any of her many palaces. This would conform to records that indicate that Hirado wares were exported to China through the offices of Chinese traders in Nagasaki.

Among this group of elaborate porcelains are several that employ extensive use of reticulation. The Amakusa clay's fine, dense, body lends itself to this type of fine piercing. Created by using shaped blades of differing sections, often almost the entire body of the object becomes an extraordinary exercise in delicate reticulation (plate 58) on a thin-walled body unsurpassed by any other kiln either in Japan or any other of the great porcelain manufacturing nations. Behind the reticulation, on the columns that support the piece internally, there are often elaborate high relief appliques sometimes in biscuit porcelain and sometimes also painted in underglaze blue. Evolving from these technical masterpieces we find the more common pieces with leaf and flower appliques. Although the best of these are of excellent technical quality, the designs are generally too cluttered to merit consideration as fine art ceramics and the worst are commercial productions of the last years of the 19th century that were made in large quantities.

Perhaps the pieces that did the most to enhance the reputation of the Hirado kilns in the 19th century were those decorated with low relief moulding. The square section koro dated 1791 illustrated in Noda II[16] and the pieces found in von Siebold's collection at Leiden that predate 1828 are conclusive proof that such techniques were in common use by the first years of the century. These relatively small pieces with simple themes are the forerunners of the more elaborate and larger examples that display the full virtues of Hirado, typified by the best of the group of flaring neck vases and other less dramatic forms. Among those that were created late in the Edo era or at the beginning of the Meiji period are the simpler vases of ovoid form that are applied with low reliefs in typical Edo taste, with native Japanese themes such as the vase

16 *pl.* 59

Plate 59

A vase painted and decorated in low relief with a cock, hen and chick beside bamboo. Early Meiji period. Height 35.0 cm

with "the four flowers" (plate 90) and another of similar form with cock, hen and chicks (plate 59). Both are of the finest white body, thickly potted and consequently very heavy. Later Meiji examples using this technique are likely to be lighter in weight, more thinly potted with a design more in keeping with new tastes that had developed subject to outside influences. The low relief vase decorated with cranes (plate 60), |datable to post 1872 because of the inscription on the base referring to Nagasaki prefecture, not created until that date], is a typical example that bears comparison with its Edo forerunners. The shape has become more complex, with an indentation towards the upper part, while the addition of two loose ring shishi head mask handles complicates the form. The combination of unrelated themes as seen on this vase — shishi, cranes and lappet borders — is typical of Meiji design. It is not often that such inconsistencies occur in Edo times. The glaze is more thinly applied and consequently shows less colour. The piece is lighter in weight, comparatively thinly potted and of extraordinarily fine quality. Such pieces typify the best Hirado of the Meiji period, and it is the Amakusa clay that makes

Plate 60
A vase decorated in low relief and blue and white with cranes walking among prunus, the handles formed as shishi masks with loose rings. The base is marked "Dai Nihon, Nagasaki ken, Mikawachi, Satomi Takeshiro" (App.6, no.79). The use of the term 'ken' (prefecture) means it must have been made after 1872 when such entities came into existence. Height 27.1 cm

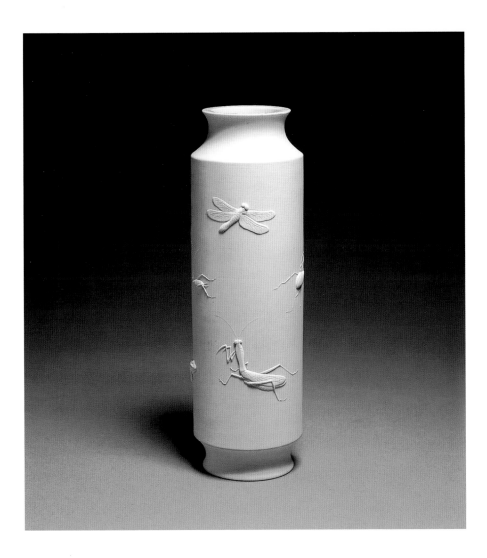

Plate 61
Plate 61
A cylindrical vase, glazed only on the interior, the exterior applied with a selection of insects in low relief. The inscription on the base (App.6, no.32) establishes this as originating from Mikawachi. Meiji period. Height 24.3 cm

Hirado ware of this era, and particularly pieces with either low or high relief sculpted decoration, so different from the products of other kilns. In firing, as already mentioned, even after the application of a thick glaze, the clay retains its sharply defined outlines and does not become blurred or "fuzzy", as with other clays.

Rarities are low-relief wares left in the biscuit on the exterior while fully glazed on the inside to ensure they are fully waterproof. Those that I have seen are made with extreme care, the edge of the glaze being meticulously finished as it meets the outside of the body and the individual appliques finely executed. Without the evidence of a cylindrical biscuit vase decorated with a wide variety of insects (plate 61), which has an incised mark on the base indicating it was made at Mikawachi, it would be open to doubt whether this small group of pieces is in fact Hirado. However, a close inspection of the the dense white paste, which is of course easily visible on biscuit wares, confirms the attribution.

Another rare type of porcelain made by the Hirado kilns were those created by Haruzane Higuchi. These thin-walled pieces are pierced with designs and the glaze allowed to fill the reticulation—a technique known among aficionados of Chinese art as "rice grain". The most celebrated of these pieces was acquired by William Walters at the end of the 19th century and remains with the rest of his collection in Baltimore. In addition to the translucent designs the vase is painted with three mythical kirins, each in a different shade of blue. Although little detail is known of individual members of the Higuchi family, they have a long association with Hirado going back to the 17th century. Riemon Higuchi (1771–1861) was famous for his decoration in relief.

Unlike the Arita kilns, Mikawachi did not make pieces of monumental proportions and the vase illustrated in plate 62, standing over 60 cm high, is among the largest known. The fact that there are so few large pieces originating in Mikawachi demonstrates that Hirado had no market for the giant vases, lanters and charges thta Arita made in such large quantities.

During the Meiji era there was a great demand for wares derived from or in the style of earlier renowned kilns such as Kakiemon, Nabeshima and even Hirado itself. This led to a significant number of commercial production centres recreating ceramics in ancient styles, often so cleverly imitating earlier versions that the two are extremely difficult to tell apart. Among the most common versions of earlier pieces are those of Nabeshima wares. These were made at many locations including the Nabeshima kilns themselves before they closed in 1871, and

subsequently by the Imaemon family when they revived the work
of their predecessors later in the century. The Hirado kilns also
made a great many dishes in Nabeshima style, though they were
not slavish in following the original designs. Most Hirado

Plate 62
*Monumental works were seldom
made at Mikawachi. Those that
exist were made no earlier than
mid 19th century. The height of
this vase with dragon handles
is 63.5 cm.*

Plates 63–65

A dish painted with a scene of fishermen beside an upturned boat prow converted to a shrine, the reverse painted in Nabeshima style with a comb foot and tasselled cash. Hokusai's design from his book The Hundred views of Fuji published between 1834 and 1845 had only to be slightly modified to fit the circular format.

In the Meiji period the Hirado kilns made many pieces with the reverse in traditional Nabeshima style though they tended to avoid exact imitations.

Diameter 15.4 cm

92

versions of Nabeshima display a reverse that is closely allied to
the original with a comb foot and tasselled cash in blue and
white. The designs on the front are generally of a type that would
not have been found in earlier times on any kind of ceramic.
Typical of these is the dish illustrated in plates 63 & 64 that takes
its design directly from one of Hokusai's "100 views of Fuji" series
of prints (plate 65). Many of the 19th century dishes currently
attributed to the Nabeshima kilns are in fact the product of the
Hirado kilns. To differentiate between the two is often difficult as
there are many similarities but telltale signs include the
whiteness of the body, the delicacy of the shading on the front,
the shape of the foot, tapering and, at the same time, slanting
inwards and the thin, mean drawing of the cash symbols and
particularly the tassels on the reverse.

Another well known example of Hirado in Nabeshima
style is the large dish [17] with a hawk in low relief on a pine branch
in the Baur collection in Geneva. Although it has been enamelled
at a later date and was originally intended to be seen only in blue
and white, this imposing dish is an artistic success in pure Hirado
style, while the reverse is traditional Nabeshima with all the
telltale signs that point to a Mikawachi origin, as detailed above.

17 III *The Baur Collection, Japanese
Ceramics E59 & Meiji, Japanese
art in transition p.94, pl.20*

Plate 66

The seven sages in the bamboo grove is a popular theme in every media in Japanese art. This example employs all the elasticity of Amakusa clay, the distinctive high fired felspathic colours of Hirado and the potter's own humour to achieve a lively group, dating from the late Edo period. Height 22.0 cm

The evolution of Hirado's sculptural works

It was the unique qualities of the Amakusa clay that enabled Hirado to create okimono, netsuke and other three dimensional sculptural works so successfully. The clay holds its form and sharply defined edges after firing, even when coated with a thick glaze, to a degree unlike any other used in the Orient. This enabled the potters to devote a significant percentage of their production to sculptural pieces and gain an enviable reputation from their success.

The first three-dimensional pieces made at Mikawachi are heavy, using large amounts of the precious clay that took so long to transport and prepare. There are only a few examples of even modest-size models dating from the 18th century; among them is a figure in the Musee Guimet, Paris, of Kuzunoha holding a leaf and seated on an Inari fox[1] which measures about 14 cms high. Another is of a seated fox and is in the Ashmolean Museum, Oxford. Both are depicted on square bases and are very heavy. The vast majority of early figures, however, are small, measuring less than 5 cms and made of solid porcelain. It is interesting to surmise why they were constructed in this way, since firing solid clay would have made it much more likely that they would distort during firing if even the slightest air bubble was left in the clay. Although it would have been harder to make moulds for hollow figures than solid ones it is unlikely this was the reason for avoiding them.

Of the three-dimensional sculptures made at Mikawachi, a wide variety of animal figures is the most commonly found. Beginning in the 18th century, they were made as devotional objects, as in the case of the foxes mentioned above, as ornaments (okimono) for display in small alcoves in the house (tokonoma) or as depictions of the representative animal of a particular year. A baku (an animal from Japanese mythology), identical to the example illustrated in plate 29, datable to 1801[2], shows beyond doubt that the kilns were making exceptional models by the the end of the century. Heavy in weight, though not entirely solid, they exhibit a powerful strength and lifelike fluidity

von Siebold: collector extra- ordinaire.

1 No.G 2642
2 *Noda 1, plate* 109. *p.*47

95

that captures the personality of a baku. Figures which probably date from a similar period are the small solid representations of boys or sages (plate 30) finely painted with patterned robes and exquisitely finished in every detail. There are fine examples of these in both the Walters Art Gallery and The Metropolitan Museum of Art.

It is to the extraordinary figure of von Siebold that we owe a debt of gratitude. Without his efforts in collecting and accumulating, we would be lacking in source material to study. His material, numbering over 7,000 pieces, was acquired during his two tours of duty stationed at Deshima Island, Nagasaki. The objects he acquired during his first stay from 1823–1828 are the most interesting for students of Hirado because all the objects acquired and inventoried at this time are conclusively datable to 1828 or before. His collection is renowned for the vast and important materials relating to the flora of Japan, but is not restricted to such narrow parameters. Among almost 5000 specimens collected during the first trip are prints, paintings, maps, books, textiles, costume, sculpture, netsuke, lacquer, combs, brushes, tools, bronzes and, of course, ceramics.

Von Siebold's collection was eventually bought by King Willem I of Holland and is housed in The National Museum of Ethnology in Leiden. Among more than 30 examples of porcelain from Mikawachi are a group of 16 netsuke which enable us to determine what was being made in the early part of the 19th century or earlier. The subject range is wide and includes animals, both mythical and real, represented in both stylised and naturalistic manners, depicting legendary and real figures in standing, seated and recumbent poses, as well as a seashell and an egg containing a scene of courting lovers just visible through an opening. The use of colour was already common at this time and is discussed more fully in chapter six. It is also clear that the kilns at Mikawachi were making netsuke in a broad range of qualities. Some of the examples in the von Siebold group are crude, some have simple artistic elegance and others a fine

Plate 67

A three case inro, ojime and netsuke, the inro painted with stylised snowflakes, the spherical ojime carved in low relief with a hare, the bead itself representing the moon, and the netsuke formed as a chrysanthemum blossom. The three separate pieces represent "the three beauties of nature", the snow in the countryside, the moon in the mountains and the flowers in the rain. At the same time each is executed in different techniques that display the finest qualities of Hirado ceramics. Hirado inro are extremely rare, the only other example known to date being in the Musee Guimet, Paris. Edo period. Length of inro 7.1 cm

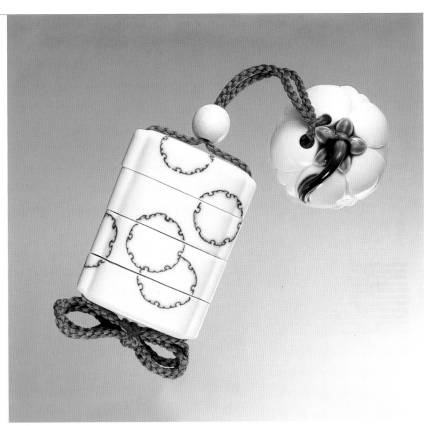

Plate 68

A netsuke formed as an eggplant decorated in underglaze blue and grey. The range of subject matter of Hirado netsuke varies widely from simple realistic miniature sculptures of fruit, flowers or vegetables to complex figural themes with moving parts. Attempting to date these netsuke is fraught with difficulty as the models were often made continuously over long periods. This example probably dates to the Edo period. Length 5.6 cm

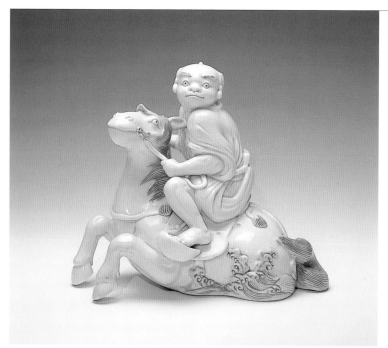

Plate 69
A large okimono of a mounted horseman emerging from water. Late Edo period. Length 18.7 cm

Plate 70
A pair of shishi and their young. From the 18th century shishi were a popular theme for the Hirado potters and it is often difficult to distinguish early from late examples. The fresh vibrant sculpture and the density of the material indicate this is more likely to belong to the Edo era rather than later. Height 30.5 cm

attention to detail and quality that demonstrates the complex and intricate techniques being undertaken by this time in Mikawachi. Loose balls that rattled in the jaws of a fierce shishi or a lion mask were popular, as were movable parts to figures. This "mobile" element features in about forty percent of the netsuke found at Leiden, suggesting such quirky features do not necessarily indicate a late date of manufacture.

An interesting group of porcelain netsuke made at Mikawachi are the models coloured to imitate ivory, often of tall standing figures. There are two unsigned examples at Leiden made from the same mould but appearing to be of different quality and character because of the different carving and finishing applied after assembly. Others of this type in later collections are signed Masakazu. These appear to be replicas of high quality ivory originals signed with the same signature of the late 18th and early 19th century Kyoto school netsuke carver whose descendants worked in Osaka. No firm link between Masakazu and Hirado has yet been discovered.

The production of netsuke was widely exploited for commercial reasons by the Hirado potters in the latter years of the 19th century. They produced large quantities of mediocre and even shoddy netsuke to sell to tourists. Both the moulding and painting are often of the lowest quality and did nothing to enhance the reputation of the kilns, but rather exploited this same reputation to its detriment. In contrast to this, a very small percentage of the production was of the highest calibre, exploring the artistic possibilities and limitations of creating netsuke in the medium of porcelain to a degree other ceramicists had not even contemplated. Like all the products of Hirado, at their best they are unsurpassed.

The development of okimono production is extremely difficult to chart as there are so few datable examples and only occasional signed pieces. The important pieces in this story are the baku already mentioned, an incense box in the form of a

Plate 71
An okimono of a deer from the same mould as the example in the Musee Guimet, Paris, both are incised with a complex inscription (App.6, no.90) establishing its date of manufacture as 1864.
Length 27.8 cm

3   GL 2115 8

4   *Private Collection*

5   *Musee Guimet & Hyatt King collection*

minogame datable to 1796, the group of netsuke and flower ornaments in Leiden known, as indicated already, to have been acquired by von Siebold prior to 1828, a water jar (the cover mounted with a stylised dragon) dated 1835, another water jar (the lid mounted with a model of a Chinese boy coloured in blue and grey) dated 1853, a white figure of a shojo by a giant sake jar[3], acquired by the Victoria & Albert Museum, London in 1855, a model of a hawk on a rockwork base dated to 1868[4] and two finely modelled figures of deer (plate 71) inscribed and dated to 1864[5]. There appear to be no other sculptural pieces of Hirado origin with verifiable dates, though more may come to light in the future.

The flower models (plates 32 & 33) are a fascinating group that at first glance appear to be akin to Victorian fancies.

Closer examination reveals a different aspect entirely. Very few of these survive intact in private hands. The examples that are undamaged are mostly to be found in public museums and have often been there for a great many years. The British Museum, The Royal Museum of Scotland, Edinburgh, Musee Guimet, Paris, The National Museum of Ethnology, Leiden, (plate 32) all have examples. Close examination reveals that they are extremely well made, with the most intricate attention to detail. The back is left unglazed to facilitate firing and presumably because it would not be seen. The application of colour, generally blue or brown but sometimes grey or celadon, is made with the utmost care, ensuring that no unwanted colour is applied.

The examples brought back from Japan by von Siebold show they were in production in the first quarter of the 19th century and most probably were being made as far back as the 18th century. As to their purpose, there have been a wide range of suggestions but it is certain that they were not merely decorations. Everything made by the Hirado potters had a purpose and use in a Japanese household, and there is no reason to suppose these were any different. The most likely use was that

Plate 72
A weight modelled as a boy seated on a raft; incised mark (App.6, no.9) to the base. Hirado made many of these charming weights from the 18th century onwards, generally of solid construction, these fine miniature sculptures often predate the Meiji era. Length 12.2 cm

101

of a ceremonial weight to be placed on top of a square cloth (fukusa) which covered a gift when a presentation was made. Only the highest ranking recipients of gifts were allowed to keep the entire package of the gift itself, the elaborate fukusa and the symbolic weight. Others could only keep the gift and had to leave the accompanying decorations. It is easy to understand that the creation of such unique ornaments would have appealed to the Matsura daimyo; what better means to create an impression than to present such a unique weight along with the gift itself? Surely the other daimyo and even the shogun would have taken note. It is likely that other figures (plate 72), often of similar oblong form, may have had the same purpose and were also intended for use as weights.

The dating of the larger animal okimono is a difficult task, The two very heavy fox figures are clearly 18th century. The charming figure of an ox accompanied by a Chinese boy (plate 73), all on an unusual slab base, also appears to be of an early date. The modelling of the boy bears a close resemblance to

Plate 73

A okimono modelled as a small boy leading an ox, all on a slab base with canted corners. This heavy model of brilliant white colour has an unusual form of base. This, together with the similarity of the small boy to early miniatures suggests an early 19th century or even 18th century date.
Height 16.5 cm

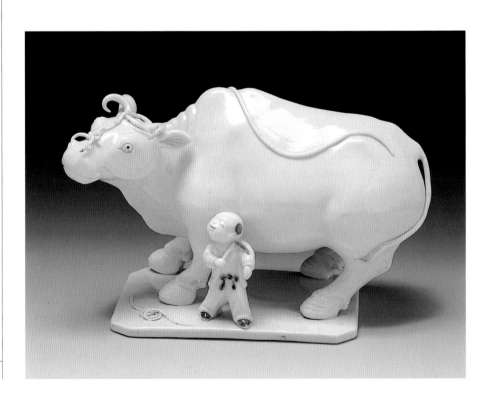

Plate 74

An okimono modelled as Kinko, scroll in hand, riding a carp, decorated in brown, grey and blue, the face and hands left unglazed. The technical comparison between this figure and the netsuke of the late Edo period is obvious. Length 16.0 cm

the small models of boys dating to the late 18th and early 19th centuries. The fat ox, a wonderful contrast to the diminutive child, is the expression of an artist's perception of an ox rather than an accurate depiction or a sentimentalised caricature, as is the case in later examples. The introduction of colour, both grey and brown, allowed the potters further scope, and although they never forgot the strong impact of pure white sculpture, they used it to good effect. The use of colour on the okimono of Kinko seated on a carp (plate 74) closely parallels its use on early 19th century netsuke, as does the style of moulding and carving, on the human figure. A similar date is more than likely.

The 19th century saw the Hirado potters develop the ceramic okimono, treating it either in a naturalistic manner or also sometimes in a more sentimental or stylised way. These pieces rarely exceed 20 cms, as in the case of the seated shishi. Figures made at Mikawachi include all the animals of the zodiac

Plate 75
An okimono formed as a seated puppy, the fur very finely incised, inscribed on the base (App.6, no.8). The extraordinary detail of this okimono is typified by the hollow bell which contains a loose rattling ball. This figure is closely related to a model of a puppy in the Victoria and Albert Museum acquired in 1885.
Length 19.0 cm

Plate 76
A large model of a seated shishi. The Hirado kilns produced many shishi models of varying sizes and qualities. This female is among the larger and more powerful examples dating from either the end of the Edo or beginning of the Meiji eras. Height 24.0 cm

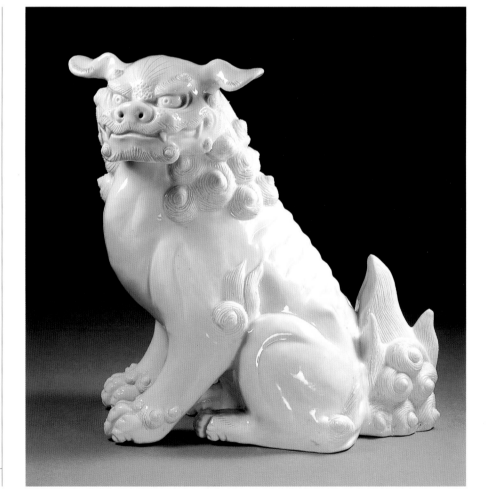

Plate 77
Fish, shells and the sea are popular themes at Hirado. The treatment of this okimono, the fish coloured in solid blue is unusual. late Edo period.
Length 21.2 cm

(rat, bull, tiger, hare, dragon, snake, horse or deer, goat, monkey, cock, dog (plate 75), boar, hawk, elephant, duck, shishi (plate 76), baku (plate 29), kirin, dragon fish as well as other fish (plate 77), images of the seven lucky gods, and of Amida Buddha (plate 78), Kannon and a variety of human subjects. The majority of Hirado okimono that come onto the market today date from the Meiji period, but some are earlier. Typically these models are hollow and have indented bases, which occasionally bear incised inscriptions identifying them as products of Hirado or Mikawachi and sometimes name the modeller responsible. Others, generally heavier in weight, have flat bases, sometimes with traces of cloth texture impressed into the clay. Although it would be interesting to surmise that the two different types of base indicate a particular chronological order of production, careful study would suggest that both types of base were made in the late Edo and Meiji eras and no firm conclusion can be drawn as to the date of models bearing either type of base structure.

Further study of okimono is needed to obtain a clear idea of the evolution of these charming and often humorous sculptures. It is to be hoped that further Edo period dated examples will be found, establishing benchmark dates.

Plate 78

A standing figure of Buddha on lotus base, his hands clasped in front holding a covered bowl; the hands and feet left in biscuit, the tightly curled hair, in grey and the mandala and bowl in brown. This is identical to another example in The Walters Art Gallery. In his catalogue of 1896 Bushell dates it to the 18th century and refers to the story of one Matsura daimyo who was cured of an illness on a pilgrimage to a shrine on the top of Mount Fuji and each year sent a retinue to the same shrine with one of these figures as a donation, which he had specially commissioned at Mikawachi.
Height 27.0 cm

There are so few dated okimono known that further information of this kind is necessary before any progress can be made in building a clear picture of the evolution of ceramic sculpture at Mikawachi.

Plate 79

A vase decorated in underglaze colours with sprays of asters, the white flowers in low relief. The three character underglaze blue mark on the base reading "Hirado yaki" (App.6, no.26) establishes the fact that this kiln made pieces decorated with a wide range of high quality underglaze colours. This technique was revived in Japan in late 19th century and this rare group of ceramics from Hirado must date after the 1880's but could have been made as late as early in the 20th century when the Fukagawa Company introduced these sophisticated techniques.
Height 26.5 cm

The development of colour on Hirado wares

To most people the word Hirado conjures up an image of fine white porcelain decorated in underglaze blue or perhaps even an object without the addition of any colour. Rarely do people associate Hirado with coloured wares. Yet closer study reveals that the kiln produced objects decorated in a wide range of colours in both overglaze and underglaze techniques. The attempt to determine the date of production of the first pieces decorated with colour is no simple task as so few pieces with firmly attributable dates exist. The earliest of these is the kogo shaped as a minogame (mythical turtle) illustrated in Noda I[1] combining the usual underglaze blue with brown and grey the box inscribed with the date 1796. Another early example may be the pair of ormolu mounted cycad plants in the collection of Her Majesty the Queen and discussed earlier in chapter 3, p.54.
A pair of 18th century dishes painted in blue with leafy tendrils, the reverse with scrolling floral patterns and the rims in brown in the Kakiemon style, are illustrated in Noda II[2]. A mid 19th century pair of plates painted with karakusa scrolls, the reverse marked Hirado san, Satomi sei (App.6, no.18) also with brown rims and illustrated in the same book[3], demonstrate the early use of colour other than blue at Hirado.

Although we have no means of pinpointing dates precisely, the group of sixteen netsuke in the National Museum of Ethnology at Leiden were acquired by Cock Blomhoff, Overmeer Fisscher and von Siebold during their residences in Japan between 1817 and 1829. Some may have been contemporary pieces but others already had some age by the time they were exported. Of the sixteen all but three have colour other than blue, most being brown or a pale shade of brown thinly applied, achieving the effect of imitating ivory. It is interesting to note that none of this group of netsuke are decorated with applied overglaze enamels but all are coloured using high-temperature felspathic coloured glazes fired at the same time as the porcelain. All are made from two-piece hollow moulds joined together and then, to various degrees hand-finished. The extent to which they are finished after being assembled determines the quality of the

Fukagawa: colourful ways.

[1]   Pl.63
[2]   Pl.339
[3]   Pl.371

Plate 80

A netsuke of a dancing boy holding a lion's head mask, coloured in blue, brown and celadon. the face and hands left unglazed. Early 19th century. Height 5.5 cm

finished product, which can range from rather crude to fine. The poorest still show marks where the two parts of the mould meet and have only the most rudimentary supplementary carving, while the finer examples show no signs of having been pieced together and have been finely chiselled to enhance their detail. Among the finest is a study of a Chinese boy standing on one leg, holding a lion mask in his hands[4]. The same model is illustrated in plate 80 showing the meticulous attention to detail and complexity of the glazes, as well as leaving parts of the features left "in the biscuit", that is, unglazed.

These pieces show that blue, brown, grey and celadon green glazes were in use by the first years of the 19th century and production in these colours is likely to have begun in the previous century. It was not only to netsuke that these colours were applied. Apart from the minogame kogo from 1796, other objects such as ceremonial weights, in the form of flower sprays and other miniature objects were decorated with colour. Among the most spectacular of these miniature sculptures is the boar sleeping in the shade of a rock beside a chrysanthemum (plate 31). This is now in The Royal Museum of Scotland, Edinburgh. It almost certainly came from the collection of Samuel Bing, which was sold by auction in Paris in 1906 after his death. Bing was a dealer in antiques, founder of the shop L' Art Nouveau in Paris and an early Hirado enthusiast. At, or around the time of the auction it was acquired by another renowned oriental enthusiast, W. Alexander, financier, philanthropist, patron of Whistler and donor of the National Portrait Gallery building in London to the nation in 1896. The boar was gifted by his daughters to the

4   *Inv. no.360–4173*

Plate 81

A *netsuke of a kneeling shishimai dancer, his mask held over his head, all in blue, brown and grey, the faces left unglazed. Early 19th century. Height 7.0 cm*

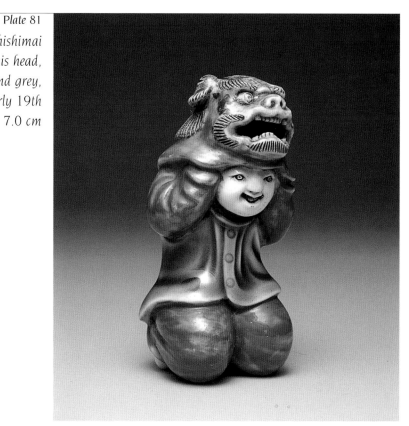

Plate 82

A *netsuke of Shoki carrying his sword, in celadon, brown, blue and grey, the face and hands unglazed. Early 19th century. Height 6.1 cm*

111

museum in 1956. Slightly larger pieces, such as the okimono of Kinko riding a carp (plate 74), were also made at this time.

A great many covered containers, the largest probably intended as water jars for the tea ceremony, formed as shells and elaborately encrusted with similar shells and other sea creatures were made at Mikawachi. The brown felspathic glaze was used to form the background colour which was interspersed with blue and white highlights. An added effect was produced by the inclusion of unglazed fragments locked within the partly open shells which would rattle when shaken. These containers were made in a range of qualities, the vast majority being of the poorer variety. It is hard to judge when production of these shell boxes began and ended but it is likely they were a common and popular series in production for much of the 19th century. Related to these is another group of figural pieces of predominantly brown colour. Although essentially decorative and often using one of the seven lucky gods as their theme, they are formed as teapots. Commonest among the divinities are Ebisu, Daikoku and Hotei which are created in a wide range of qualities, often competing with each other to show the most ingenious form of spout and handle that could be interpreted as a natural phenomenon. The best possess a vivacity and humorous expression that gives them an appeal only found in Hirado wares.

None of the pieces we have so far discussed have overglaze colours. There are however examples of 18th century blue and white Hirado with added enamels[5]; perhaps even added in Arita near to the time of manufacture, but these are essentially finished items that were then further embellished. This is a phenomenon often encountered with Oriental ceramics, the enamels being added either locally or, as in the case of some Arita wares, applied in Holland, far away. It is not my intention to discuss such "clobbered" wares in this book.

The earliest firmly datable example of Hirado ware decorated with overglaze colours is the fine quality baluster vase

[5]   *Noda II, pl. 336*

on flaring foot (App.6, no.92) with carved biscuit decoration, now in the Victoria and Albert Museum. It was made in 1875 for the Philadelphia Exhibition the following year and enamelled and gilded to a high technical standard. Aside from the bright colouration, one would have no doubt that it was made at Mikawachi and this is confirmed by an impressed circular mark on the base reading "dai Nihon Mikawachi sei". More surprising is the second mark in red enamel, "Koransha ni oite, Nishiyama sei", indicating that it was decorated by Seizan at the Koransha studios. Clearly it is a vase made at Mikawachi and then enamelled at Koransha and is the first evidence we have of the link between Hirado and the Koransha studios, later to become part of the Fukagawa Company. This relates to the earlier statement that the eggshell export table wares that had been produced earlier in the century were already being enamelled by this time at workshops outside the Mikawachi boundaries.

Among those pieces likely to have been made earlier in the century and enamelled either at the kilns themselves or at a workshop close by are the very fine figures of the Emperor and Empress of Japan (plates 83 and 84). Of heavy, almost solid

Plates 83 & 84
A pair of enamelled figures of the Emperor and Empress. Possibly enamelled outside the official Mikawachi kiln, these highly detailed okimono were probably intended as gifts for the Imperial family in the late 18th or early 19th century. Height of Emperor 9.9 cm

Plate 85
*An okimono modelled as a
hare, the markings and
hair work painted in gold,
the eyes in black, the base
incised (App.6, no.46).
The Musee Guimet, Paris
houses a number of
similarly gilded Hirado
models decorated in
overglaze colours of different
types dating from the early
Meiji period.
Length 19.0 cm*

construction akin to other models of the early part of the 19th
century, these meticulously made and carefully decorated figures
certainly predate the vase in the Victoria and Albert Museum and
it is likely that they were in fact made by the Matsura daimyo for
presentation to the Emperor. The palette is more akin to that
used on Arita porcelains in the late 18th century than that on
the 1875 vase or indeed the palette used on Fukagawa export
production later in the century. It is known that Mukuo Saisuke
and Mukuo Jonosuke were enamelists at Mikawachi in 1835 and it
could be that these figures were decorated by one of these artists.

Another enamelled vase known conclusively to exist
before the end of the last century is in The Walters Art Gallery and
published by Bushell in his catalogue of the collection in 1896[6],
where he dates it to the 18th century. The simple bulbous form
with elongated cylindrical neck is extravagantly embellished with

mythical animal head handles. The central area is broken by a band of incised stylised waves in typical Hirado fashion and the decoration, all in overglaze colour, consists of scrolling foliage on a russet ground. If the vase had been decorated in blue or left plain there would have been no difficulty in suggesting a late 18th or early 19th century date.

A further group of enamelled wares mostly of animal okimono have recently come to light in the storage areas of the Musee Guimet. Although it has been impossible to gain proper access due to the extensive refurbishment of the museum which will take some years, it is likely that most of these were acquired in the last quarter of the 19th century by Grandidier and certainly before the latter's death in 1908. The range of enamelling varies from simple gilding and use of Kutani style iron red to brocade patterns, possibly applied later than the date of manufacture. This interesting group may well shed light on the dating of enamelled wares once further research has been carried out.

Plate 86
A yellow glazed model of a recumbent horse. This model, more commonly seen in white demonstrates that nothing was beyond the capability or imagination of the Hirado potters. Length 16.0 cms

In spite of the existence of the marks mentioned above and other overglaze inscriptions identifying Hirado porcelain as originating in its kilns, it is not clear which overglaze enamelling was actually carried out at the Hirado kilns themselves. There appears to be no means of knowing the precise quantities of ceramics enamelled at the official kiln as opposed to workshops nearby. By 1841 a workshop had been established at Mikawachi[7], under the aegis of Hisatomi Yajibei, the wealthy Arita merchant from Nakanohara, expressly for the purpose of decorating with overglaze enamels. The main reason was to supply colourfully decorated eggshell table wares to the Dutch traders in Nagasaki. Large quantities of pieces were made and marked "Zoshuntei Sampo".

Another workshop decorating Hirado eggshell wares was founded in 1871 or 1872 after the abolition of the Han system and the introduction of present day prefectures. Known as The Nagasaki Hirado Trading Company its pieces are marked "Manpozan Shoho", "Hirado san, Giei zo" or "Manpozan, Giei sei".

Often of dubious artistic merit, though by no means always, these cups and saucers are made of the finest eggshell porcelain, featherweight and extremely translucent, decorated in bright enamels with subjects ranging from birds and flowers to samurai and geisha. Production continued for many years, at least well into the Meiji period, the colour schemes becoming more gaudy as the years progressed. A single cup could have up to seven different coloured enamels, as well as gold, making it an expensive item. Others were decorated in the red and gold of the Kutani palette, always a popular colour scheme for the export market as can be seen in the European shaped cup in this colour scheme, signed on the base with a Hirado mark.

The relationship between The Fukagawa Company, or its predecessor Koransha, and Hirado is not clear. We know that it was already established by 1875 when they jointly made a vase for the Philadelphia exhibition. We know of undecorated animal okimono identical to marked Hirado examples that bear

7   *Brinkley*

Plate 87
A reticulated koro on three feet
decorated in underglaze blue and
brown with enamelled green and
red with ho-o in roundels,
the pierced cover of leafy design
highlighted in underglaze blue,
grey and pink, the borders gilded
with scrolling patterns and
Tokugawa emblems. Marked
(App.6, no.95) on the base in red
"Keimei" with seal. This interesting
koro poses more questions than
it answers! The form, though
slightly larger than average
suggests an early to mid 18th
century date as does the design.
The presence of underglaze grey
and pink which are known to
have been introduced late in the
century appear to rule out this
possibility suggesting that it is
more likely made circa 1800.
Height 9.0 cm

impressed Fukagawa marks. We know of reticulated koros
decorated with typical Fukagawa enamels with the underglaze
blue Mount Fuji rebus, the trademark of the Fukagawa Company.
But we do not know the precise nature of this relationship.
It has been suggested that in the first years of the 20th century,
Fukagawa took over or absorbed the Hirado kilns into its
operation, but I can find no conclusive evidence to support this.
It is more likely that the Mikawachi kilns produced blanks to order
for decoration by Fukagawa and at the same time continued to
make both plain and blue and white items for the commercial
market. There are too many Hirado pieces, clearly datable to the
first quarter of the 20th century, available on the market today to
allow us to presume that the production of Hirado wares ceased
entirely in the first years of the 20th century.

A third category of coloured wares made at Hirado
exists. Technically different from either of the two groups
discussed above, they appear to be akin to the underglaze
coloured wares developed by Makuzu Kozan and others,

Plate 88

A vase decorated in underglaze colours with a continuous design of irises, the base marked "Hirado yaki" (App.6, no.25). Meiji period. Height 24.0 cm

Plate 89

A flower vase on four feet with wide flaring lip painted in blue with floral roundels and in underglaze red with dragons, the lower part with low relief stylised wave patterns. The low relief work and the exaggerated form of the upper part of the vase owe their success to the plastic properties of the Amakusa clay. These together with the soft shading of the blue and the superbly controlled underglaze red that the kiln introduced in their later years make this a unique and distinctly Hirado piece. Height 18 cm

118

reaching the pinnacle of their prowess between 1890 and 1910.
These fine porcelains, generally of simple, elegant shape,
are decorated in underglaze colours of the highest quality. At first
glance they appear to be far from the traditional products of
Hirado; yet on close examination they have a pure white paste
and a thick, slightly tinted, soft glaze that is entirely typical. There
are only a handful of these Hirado wares with underglaze colour
bearing Hirado marks known to exist. The vase with raised aster
design (plate 79) shows other typical Hirado characteristics and
had it been executed solely in blue and white (and unmarked),
one could have come to no other conclusion than that it was
from Mikawachi. The vase decorated with irises, together with
another pierced vase decorated with a carp in underglaze grey,
appears to have a stylistic affinity with Fukagawa, yet the marks
on both identify them as Hirado. In view of the relationship
between these two organisations, this is no surprise. There are
a great many pieces of unmarked porcelain decorated with
underglaze colours and it would be tempting to ascribe the origin
of some of these to Hirado. However, unless there are other very
distinct characteristics that lead to the conclusion that they are
Hirado, it would be irresponsible to suggest such an origin.
It is clear that Hirado made only a few of these coloured wares
that rival the products of the well-known studio ceramic artists.
It appears that there are no "lesser" wares or developmental
pieces and that there are no clues as to how the skills were
developed to create such fine underglaze wares. This would
suggest that the expertise was brought in from outside their own
resources, certainly influenced by the German chemist Gottfried
Wagener who did much to develop underglaze colours in Japan.
In view of the existing relationship these skills could have come
from the artisans at Fukagawa.

Plate 90

A vase painted and decorated in low relief with the "four king flowers". The symbolism of the flowers; the chrysanthemum, prunus bamboo and orchid alludes to the harmony of nature when depicted together. Although vases of simple form such as this are found in Western collections, either acquired close to the time of manufacture in the early Meiji period or at a later date, they were nevertheless intended for use in Japan. Height 35.8 cm

20th century collectors

Soame Jenyns: scholar and enthusiast.

The famous kilns of Japan are well established among connoisseurs and collectors world wide. Names such as Kutani, Kakiemon and Nabeshima instantly bring to mind ceramics of quality, rarity and high value, often the subject of intense competition. Seldom nowadays is Hirado thought of in the same terms and one must ask why. Has Hirado always been thought of as secondary to the great names, or is this a more recent phenomenon? Certainly the great Western collectors of the 19th and even the early 20th century—Brinkley, Walters, Guimet, Grandidier, Baur, Bing, Franks, Tomkinson, many of whom have been mentioned in this volume—held Hirado in the highest esteem. Authors of this era, too, were almost unanimous in their praise for the merits of Hirado and so it is surprising to find that later in the century Hirado is often regarded as a second rate kiln of limited merit and little historical importance.

The depression of the 1930's and the World War that followed had a significant impact on the world collector's market, depressing prices and reducing interest. This was particularly true for almost all items of Japanese origin. To the West, after all, Japan was the enemy. In addition the commercial Japanese products made for sale to the world's markets after the war were cheap, poorly made and mass produced. It was assumed, incorrectly, that everything made in Japan was of a similar nature. It is not surprising then that after the war the interest in things Japanese took several years to gather momentum and it was not until the 1950's that interest in Japanese porcelain was stimulated by a small group of English collectors. Names such as de la Mare, Barrett, Soame Jenyns, Gerald Reitlinger and Wingfield Digby are now well know for their interest in Japanese ceramics, in particular. One cannot know why but they only had a limited interest in the merits of Hirado. Perhaps it was the scarcity and the fact that Europe's great country houses and particularly those in Britain were crammed with the finest Imari and Kakiemon. The great museums had wonderful collections from these kilns, as well as Nabeshima and the occasional example of Kutani, but little Hirado. [Much of Franks' collection that he bequeathed to the British Museum was deacquisitioned in the 1940's]. The market was awash with fine and rare pieces from the recognised major kilns and it appeared that unlike their forbears, these more recent collectors did not rank Hirado highly.

There were few books on Japanese ceramics apart from Bushell's and Brinkley's excellent and largely accurate volumes. Audsley and Bowes had earlier all published works whose reliability had come into question. It was against this background that the new generation of enthusiasts arose. In 1965 Soame Jenyns published his definitive book, "Japanese Porcelain", undertaking monumental work to write the first comprehensive English-language study on the history of the numerous porcelain kilns of Japan. Much of his effort, like the scope of his own

Plate 91
A teapot and cover painted with cranes flying among snow laden willow trees. The fuller, highly meticulous decoration suggests an early 19th century date for this elegant utensil destined for the Matsura home. Height 10.2 cm

collecting, was directed towards Kakiemon, Kutani, Imari and Arita, and these take up the bulk of his book. The information available to Jenyns at that time was quite limited, as interest in ceramics within Japan itself was small and the excavations in Arita that have recently been carried out had yet to take place. Apart from providing detailed information about chronology and dating porcelain, researches later also come to prove that the early green Kutani wares, that were considered to originate in Kaga, were in fact made at Arita. Drawing on the sources available to him, Soame Jenyns refers to Hirado as "a fine white, or blue and white, porcelain made at or near Mikawachi in the village of Use, Nagasaki Ken, in the latter part of the eighteenth century and the first thirty years of the nineteenth century from the porcelain clay of the Amakusa Island". Although sketchily referring to the earlier origins of the kilns and stating that "from 1751 to 1843 the finest porcelain in Japan was made at Mikawachi",

Plate 92

This plain white flower vase of diamond shaped section imitates the wooden well heads often seen in rural Japan. Interestingly the original wooden box has been made in the same shape to ensure a snug fit. Length 33.0 cm

123

Plate 93
A sake bottle of square section painted with panels of boys chasing butterflies among peonies emerging from rocks, the short neck surrounded by petals in low relief, the flat base unglazed.
Height 26.4 cm

the thrust of the writing was to portray Hirado as a lesser kiln with little historical importance.

It is in this context that modern collectors have come to view Hirado and I hope that this book has gone some way to correct this perception. Not only were the best Hirado wares of the highest technical and artistic quality, but the founders of these kilns also played an important role in establishing the porcelain industry in Japan. This underestimation of the role Hirado played in the early years of the Japanese porcelain industry has been a significant reason for the lack of interest in its wares.

Arita and Kakiemon were much larger scale concerns whose production was numerically far superior to Hirado. The Dutch East India Company records mention of thousands, even tens of thousands, of pieces of Imari being exported at a time. Their production in the 17th and 18th century alone must have numbered millions of pieces. Although there are indeed shapes and designs that are rare and were only made in very small numbers, the vast majority of items were produced in repeated or related patterns in the thousands. This standardisation has an obvious appeal to anyone collecting variants or different versions

Plate 94
A sake bottle of double gourd form painted with a continuous scene of boys chasing butterflies beneath a pine tree. This bottle displays the creative invention of the decorator. Faced with the problem of having no painting on the upper part of this piece he has cleverly twisted the branch of the pine tree by 270° filling the blank area in the upper part.
Height 21.5 cm

to build an interesting and representative group. Hirado's production was of an entirely different nature. Small in scale, (it is reputed that firings in the early years took place only every six months), the product were made for the private use of an extended family. What use had they for the hundreds of identical dishes that were the commercial life blood of the Arita potters? What use for the giant jars and covers, even garnitures, that were to sit so elegantly in the halls of Europe's great houses? Hirado made pieces in small quantities; one's, two's, ten's. Rarely do we find large numbers of identical items. Patterns are seldom repeated precisely; rather, we see new versions of a pattern on an alternative shape. Hirado concentrated on the individually made item. Even after 1843 when the kilns were producing commercially, it appears that they followed the same philosophy and today only rarely do more than one or two duplicates appear on the market. Perhaps the exception to this is the "boys chasing butterflies" pattern that became almost Hirado's trademark. This pattern was made continuously from the 18th century on a wide variety of shapes and can be commonly found in the full breadth of qualities from intricately detailed to sloppily sketchy.

Plate 95

An incense box (kogo) formed as an open chestnut coloured in celadon and brown. Kogo were an essential part of the tea ceremony and this small box was probably made for use by the Matsura family to use, prior to the kiln's change to a commercial operation in 1843. Maximum length 8.9 cm

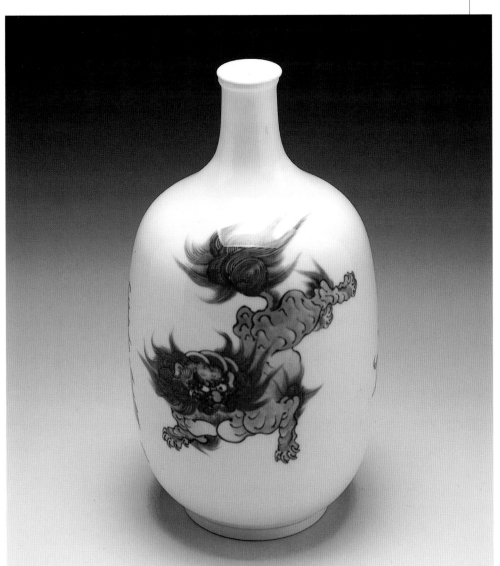

Plate 96
A sake bottle painted with a frolicking shishi with an almost human face, the reverse with a pomegranate branch. The shape of this bottle was in common usage in the late 19th and early 20th centuries. The single lively shishi occupying the central space creates a useful and attractive object. The inscription on the base (App.6, no.80) indicates that this vase was given as third prize at the Great Japanese Industrial exhibition in 1903.
Height 22.9 cm

While the quantities made were much less than from the Arita kilns, the range of forms far exceeded that of any other porcelain-making kiln. To the standard range of shapes made at Arita, all the forms necessary for tea ceremony, as well as Hirado's famous range of okimono and netsuke, must be added. For example, an incense box (kogo) which was made in few forms at Arita can be found in circular, globular, square, rectangular, fan, interlocking fan, drum, hexagonal, octagonal, bow, petal, shell, tama, duck, goose, minogame and chestnut (plate 95) form in

Plate 97

*A koro formed as a
recumbent elephant,
a section of the back pierced
and removable. Elephants
were a popular theme in
Kyushu in the late Edo period
as they were occasionally
imported through the port of
Nagasaki. Both in paintings
and three dimensional
representations Japanese
artists usually created a
striking stylisation rather
than a realistic impression of
the animal. Width 25 cm*

Hirado ware. And no doubt there are more! In total, there are
hundreds of forms to be added to the hundreds of different types
of decoration.

The individuality of each piece is further accentuated
by the eccentricities of Hirado. The ware seems to refuse to be
bound by conventions or categorisation. There always seems to
be another unique shape appearing on the market that has not
yet been recorded. Often it is not only a rarity but a worthwhile
piece adding a further dimension to the scope of Hirado.
The individual potter's or painter's sense of humour can often be
seen—the quirky look on a shishi's face (plate 96), the eccentric
posture of an elephant (plate 97), the knowing look between the
figures of Shoki and an oni, or simply the eccentric design of a
wasp's nest on a dish (plate 98) intended for delicacies—all

elements not to be found in larger-scale productions. This is a very different picture from the more easily definable Arita, Imari and Kakiemon. It is therefore understandable that collectors found it more difficult to assimilate a clear picture of the style of the Hirado kiln's wares.

Most recent collectors therefore largely ignored Hirado, writing it off as "late" or "export ware", often justifying their view by pointing to the fresh, sparkling look of the glaze and body in contrast to the duller tones of Arita. The unique designs were thought to have been for the export market, as so little was known of the history of the kiln. The sculpture was erroneously regarded by many as being intended for the drawing rooms of the late Victorians, rather than the gifts of an important daimyo.

Plate 98

A dish of double gourd form encrusted with leaves in high relief and painted in blue with wasps swarming round their nest. Made during the early part of the 19th century, this dish, probably one of a set of five, was intended for serving delicacies. Length 18.6 cm

The truth that the kiln's tradition was more akin to that of the only other private porcelain kiln in Japan, Nabeshima. Nabeshima has long been one of the most admired porcelains, commanding high prices and collected throughout the world. Nowadays growing interest in Hirado has brought more pieces to the market and it is also beginning to claim its rightful respect among the

Plate 99
A *bottle vase painted with a tiger in a bamboo grove.* Height 22.9 cm

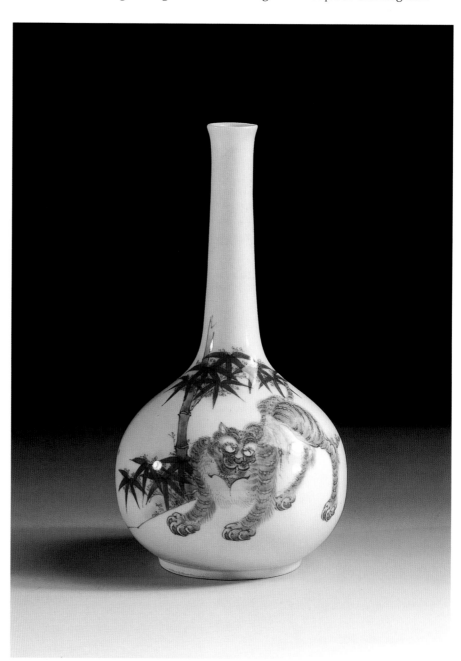

Plate 100
A water jar with panels depicting cranes over waves, cock and hen, plovers and crabs between finely sculpted masks on an incised geometric ground. Hirado made more water jars than any other porcelain manufacturing kiln. Initially simple in form they became more elaborate toward the end of Edo period reflecting the new demand for more complex pieces. Height 22.9 cm

highest ranks of Japanese kilns. It is to be hoped that its new, higher profile will continue to further its reputation and establish its place in history. There can be no doubt that Hirado was indeed porcelain for princes and that it is a prince of porcelains.

Plate 101

A reticulated vase painted with irises beneath a lappet border. The theme and execution of this vase suggest a Fukagawa origin.
The underglaze mark (App.6, no.45) however reads "Mikawachi, Imabo sei" confirming it was made at the Hirado kilns. Meiji period.
Height 23.0 cm

The lineage of the Matsura family

Born	Died	Name	Generation
822	895	Toru (Sasho)	Founder
859	918	Noboru (Asho)	2
891	942	Tsukau (Bushu)	3
933	953	Mitsuru (Mita)	4
953	1025	Tsuna (Watanabe)	5
		Sazuku (Nagoya)	6
		Yusushi (Takiguchi)	7
1064	1148	Hisashi (Matsura)	8
		Naoshi (Mikuriya)	9
		Hiraku (Mine)	10
		Tamotsu (Teruyama)	11
		Tsunagu (Hirado)	12
		Tatau (Shinsei)	13
		Kotou (Gengo)	14
		Sadamu (Hishu)	15
		Suguru (Kokushi)	16
		Osamu (Ansei)	17
		Naoshi (Shoei)	18
		Suguru (Shorin)	19
		Yoshi (Shunko)	20
	1470	Yoroshi (Tenso)	21
	1479	Toyohisa (Ten'o)	22
1466	1515	Hirosada (Kakuo)	23
	1541	Okinobu (Korei)	24
1529	1599	Takanobu (Doka)	25
1549	1614	Shigenobu (Hoin)	26
1571	1602	Hisanobu (Taigaku)	27
1591	1637	Takanobu (Soyo)	28
1622	1703	Chinshin (Tensho)	29
1646	1713	Takashi (Yuko)	30
1684	1756	Atsunobu (Shoei)	31
1710	1728	Arinobu (Tokaku)	32
1712	1779	Sanenobu (Ansei)	33
1760	1841	Kiyoshi (Seizan)	34
1791	1867	Hiromu (Kanchu)	35
1812	1858	Terasu (Taijo)	36
1840	1908	Akira (Shingetsu)	37
1864	1934	Atushi (Ranshu)	38
1884	1962	Susumu (Nyogetsu)	39
1912	1981	Motomu (Shogetsu)	40
1941		Akira (Kogetsu)	41

Known kiln sites and their sizes within the borders of the Hirado fief.

Name	Site	(metres) width	depth
1. Nakano	Hiradoshi, Yamanaka-machi, Kamisuki	2	2
2. Tsurugamine	Hiradoshi, Iwanoue-machi		
3. Nagahayama	Saseboshi, Mikawachi, Maeda Tatara	1.8	
4. Mikawachi-shimo	Saseboshi, Mikawachi, Ichinoma		
5. Yoshinata-oku	Saseboshi, Mikawachi, Ichinoma		
6. Kanabayashi	Saseboshi, Mikawachi, Kanabayashi	3.10	3.40
7. Furutani	Saseboshi, Mikawachi, Kotani	5.2	3.5
8. Sugibayashi	Saseboshi, Mikawachi, Sugibayashi		
9. Kuguriishi	Saseboshi, Mikawachi, Kuguriishi		
10. Mikawachi-nishi	Saseboshi, Mikawachi, Nakadori		
11. Mikawachi-higashi	Saseboshi, Mikawachi, Kongotsuji-Itaya	8.2	4.2
12. Yamanokami	Saseboshi, Mikawachi, Kongotsuji-Itaya		
13. Kamiryosen-higashi	Saseboshi, Mikawachi, Kamiryosen	8.4	6.2
14. Kamiryosen-nishi	Saseboshi, Mikawachi, Kamiryosen	4.2	3.5
15. Ushiishi	Saseboshi, Sin'ikue-cho, Ushiishi	2.0	2.0
16. Enaga-Furu (A)	Saseboshi, Enaga-machi, Yokotani	7.0	5.0
16a - (B)	Saseboshi, Enaga-machi, Yokotani	6.2	5.08
16b - (C)	Saseboshi, Enaga-machi, Yokotani	5.0	4.7
17. Enaga-higashi	Saseboshi, Enaga-cho, Deguchitani	7.2	4.0
18. Enaga-nishi	Saseboshi, Enaga-machi, Enagaguchi		
19. An-no-yoko	Saseboshi, Kihara-cho, Jizodaira	2.0	2.0
20. An-no-mae	Saseboshi, Kihara-cho, Sarayama		

Name	Site	(metres) width	depth
21. Jizodaira-nishi	Saseboshi, Kihara-cho, Jizodaira	3.19	3.0
22. Jizodaira-higashi	Saseboshi, Kihara-cho, Jizodaira	4.13	4.1
23. Kihara-nishi	Saseboshi, Kihara-cho, Kamanotani		
24. Kiharatani	Saseboshi, Kihara-cho, Kamanotani		
25. Kihara-shimo	Saseboshi, Kihara-cho, Kamanotani		
26. ihara-higashi	Saseboshi, Kihara-cho, Kannondaira	10.0	8.0
27. Yanaginomoto	Saseboshi, Kihara-cho, Odori		
28. Yoshinomoto (1)	Saseboshi, Kihara-cho, Yoshinomoto	2.2	2.2
28a - (2)	Saseboshi, Kihara-cho, Yoshinomoto	2.21	2.22
28b - (3)	Saseboshi, Kihara-cho, Yoshinomoto	2.54	2.85
29. Fujiwara	Saseboshi, Kurokami-cho, Fujiwara	3.5	3.5
30. Hirota (1)	Saseboshi, Hirota-cho, Ote	4.2	4.2
30a - (2)	Saseboshi, Hirota-cho, Ote	4.0	3.6
31. Sasa-Ichinose	Kitamatsura-gun, Sasa-machi, Ichinose	7.0	

List of dated or datable Hirado pieces with location, if known

All pieces known to the author to be datable prior to 1868 have been included, examples of later dates have been included only when they establish a benchmark date.

Date	Object	Location	Illustrated
1624	Vase with inscription	Tsuragamine Castle Museum	Jenyns plate 2b
1723	Set 5 dishes painted flowers	Noda, Kudo & others	plate 11
1743	Water jar and cover, undecorated		Noda II pl.51
1759	Bowls & covers, floating flowers		Noda II pl.333
1772	Cylindrical tripod censer	Hyatt King collection	App.6, no.83
1784	*Bowl & lid, autumn grasses		C.T.[1] Issue 241
1787	*Tea bowl, boys & peonies	Kyushu Porc. Cultural Mus	
1791	Square koro, relief decoration	Kyushu Porc. Cultural Mus	Noda I pl.59
1796	*Minogame shaped kogo		Noda I pl.63
1801	*Pair baku okimono		Noda I pl.109
1808	Plate, geese among reeds (93.3.348)	Metropolitan Museum	TOCS pl.9 no.16
1819	Koro with inscription		Noda II pl.104
1821	*Tea bowl with boys/butterflies	Kyushu Porc. Cultural Mus	
1824	Dish, boys and Matsura mon		NTT[2] 182
Pre 1828	Netsuke—white shishi (360–2200)	Natl. Mus. of Ethnology, Leiden	Andon vol.30
Pre 1828	Netsuke—white shishi on ball (1–2665)	Natl. Mus. of Ethnology, Leiden	Andon vol.30

Date	Object	Location	Illustrated
Pre 1828	Netsuke—brown shishi (360–4180)	Natl. Mus. of Ethnology, Leiden	Andon vol.30
Pre 1828	Netsuke—brown dog with puppy (1–2662)	Natl. Mus. of Ethnology, Leiden	Andon vol.30
Pre 1828	Netsuke—horse with black mane (360–4182)	Natl. Mus. of Ethnology, Leiden	Andon vol.30
Pre 1828	Netsuke—blue monkey (1–2666)	Natl. Mus. of Ethnology, Leiden	Andon vol.30
Pre 1828	Netsuke—boy on ox, mock ivory (360–481)	Natl. Mus. of Ethnology, Leiden	Andon vol.30
Pre 1828	Netsuke—brown deity on deer (1–2657)	Natl. Mus. of Ethnology, Leiden	Andon vol.30
Pre 1828	Netsuke—brown sennin (360–4179)	Natl. Mus. of Ethnology, Leiden	Andon vol.30
Pre 1828	Netsuke—sennin, mock ivory (360–4171)	Natl. Mus. of Ethnology, Leiden	Andon vol.30
Pre 1828	Netsuke—blue & black sennin (360–4178)	Natl. Mus. of Ethnology, Leiden	Andon vol.30
Pre 1828	Netsuke—brown standing sennin (1–2662)	Natl. Mus. of Ethnology, Leiden	Andon vol.30
Pre 1828	Netsuke—ivory standing sennin(360–4163)	Natl. Mus. of Ethnology, Leiden	Andon vol.30

Date	Object	Location	Illustrated
Pre 1828	Netsuke—blue, celadon, black, brown, biscuit Chinese boy (360–4173)	Natl. Mus. of Ethnology, Leiden	Andon vol.30
Pre 1828	Netsuke—white egg w. lovers (360–4157)	Natl. Mus. of Ethnology, Leiden	Andon vol.30
Pre 1828	Netsuke—brown clamshell (360–4162)	Natl. Mus. of Ethnology, Leiden	Andon vol.30
Pre 1828	White sake cup with turtle model (1–653)	Natl. Mus of Ethnology, Leiden	AJ p.57, pl.69
Pre 1828	Weight—chestnut branch (1–2650)	Natl. Mus. of Ethnology, Leiden	AJ p.97, pl.117
Pre 1828	Koro & cover—boys (1–1701)	Natl. Mus. of Ethnology, Leiden	AJ p.98, pl.118
Pre 1828	Dish with handle— morning glory(1–565)	Natl. Mus. of Ethnology, Leiden	AJ p.99, pl.119
Pre 1828	Chaire— hawthorn/cracked ice (1–489)	Natl. Mus. of Ethnology, Leiden	AJ p.1–, pl.120
Pre 1828	White low relief koro & cover (1–1804)	Natl. Mus. of Ethnology, Leiden	TOCS p.18, pl.13
Pre 1828	Bowl & cover, landscape (1–488)	Natl. Mus of Ethnology, Leiden	TOCS p.18, pl.14
Pre 1828	White low relief hibachi (1–493)	Natl. Mus. of Ethnology, Leiden	TOCS p.19, pl.15
1834	Inscribed everted bowl		Noda I pl.245
1835	Ink stone	Nagasaki Pref. Art Museum	Noda I pl.111
1835	Bottle vase, boys & Wakigawa crest	Private collection, USA	S³ p.104
1835	Cylindrical spill vase, vines		Noda I pl.139
1835	Cylindrical brush pot	Hyatt King collection	Plate 25

Date	Object	Location	Illustrated
1835	Covered bowl, morning glory		Noda II pl.303
1836	Cup stand, tortoises		Noda I pl.175
1836	*Set bowls & covers, boys/butterflies		Noda I pl.225
1838	*Bowl, boys	Nagasaki Pref. Art Museum	
1844	*Water jar, landscape		Noda I pl.41
1846	*Bowl & cover, geese and reeds		Noda I pl.226
1852	Brush washer, crane and turtles		Noda I pl.124
1853	Water jar, sages painting, boy finial		App.6, no.89
Pre 1853	White shojo and sake jar okimono (GL2115)	Victoria & Albert Museum	
1854	*Sake bottle, chrysanthemums		Noda I pl.150
1859	Large inscribed koro		Noda I pl.60
1864	White deer okimono	Hyatt King collection	plate 71
1864	White deer okimono	Musee Guimet	
1866	Cup stand, landscape	Nagasaki Pref. Art Museum	
1868	White hawk on rock work base	Private Collection UK	
1874	White tiger okimono		Noda I pl.104
1875	Enamelled vase (361.77)	Victoria & Albert Museum	App.6, no.92
Pre 1885	Puppy okimono	Victoria & Albert Museum	
1887	*Shell form container and lid	Kagedo, Seattle	KJA[4] p.27 no.22
1907	Vase with relief phoenix in clouds		AWC[5]

*= these pieces are unmarked but have original boxes with inscriptions containing a date.

[1]   Chiisani tsubomi (a magazine for collectors of Japanese antiques)

[2]   Catalogue of Nagasaki-no-Toji Tokubetsu-ten (Showa 63)

[3]   Sotheby's, London, March 1990

[4]   Shadowed Reflections, Japanese Views. A catalogue by Kagedo Japanese Art, 1997

[5]   Art of World Ceramics—vol 8 by T. Nagatake, S. Hayashi & H. Nishida, Tokyo 1978

Analyses of Porcelain Materials from various sources

	I. Amaku-saishi	II. Kutani-ishi	III. Tono-kuchiishi	IV. Kaseda	V. VI. VII. Porcelain-stones from the quarries of Kimönnhsien, at Kingtetschin, in China.			VIII. IX. Pegmatite from Yükan, in China.		X. Pegma-tite from St. Yrieix.
Silicic acid	73.87	76.60	78.72	77.15	74.77	75.42	77.75	74.70	77.00	74.99
Alumina	15.25	14.75	14.51	13.50	16.29	16.45	15.38	15.70	15.00	14.80
Ferric oxide	0.73	0.86	traces	0.94	—	—	—	—	—	0.37
Manganic oxide	—	—	"	—	—	—	—	0.10	—	—
Lime	0.43	0.29	"	0.83	2.61	0.74	1.26	0.10	0.20	1.09
Magnesia	—	—	0.42	0.62	—	—	—	0.20	—	0.36
Potash	5.46	3.91	0.39	3.34	2.81	2.45	3.32	⎱6.40	4.70	⎱4.31
Sodium oxide	1.07	0.65	—	1.85	2.05	2.34	—	⎰		⎰3.49
Water	2.23	2.68	5.34	1.64	2.42	2.74	2.51	2.40	2.40	0.65
	99.04	99.74	99.38	99.87	100.95	100.14	100.22	99.60	99.30	100.06

Reproduced from *The Industries of Japan* by J.J. Rein (New York, 1889)

Identifying and dating Hirado

Since Hirado wares became recognised as a significant group of ceramics, commanding prices higher than the wares of other minor kilns, auctioneers, dealers and collectors alike have been tempted to attribute many and various wares to the Hirado kilns. It is entirely understandable that this should happen, as there have been no books or guidelines on the subject. I hope that this book will go some way to discourage these over hopeful attributions. Identifying Hirado is often difficult and made more so by other kilns' making their own products in Hirado style, both in the 18th century and in more recent times.

The Hirado kilns made small quantities of pieces for the personal use of the Matsura daimyo, as well as a larger production of items for use by other lesser members of his entourage. In the 19th century, yet others were made for commercial sale. Those from the latter two groups are often of significantly inferior quality and so a piece should not be discounted as having a Hirado origin on the grounds of lack of quality. However, a Hirado attribution to such a piece does not increase its merit.

GLAZES

There is wide difference in the colour of Hirado glazes throughout the kiln's long history, but there appears to be no firm chronological progression of glaze colour changes. Consequently, attempting to date a piece solely on the grounds of glaze colour is unwise. Even pairs, obviously fired at the same time, can have significantly different glaze colours, simply because the two pieces were immersed in different buckets of glaze. When applied thickly, the glaze used at Mikawachi has a noticeable hue, generally either yellowish or greenish, though examples with a bluish hue are not unknown. When applied thinly the glaze colour becomes less pronounced and almost colourless. These glaze colours are evident throughout the history of production.

Early Hirado wares have a softness to the glaze and a marked green or grey-greenish hue that diminishes in the 19th century. This early, very finely textured glaze reflects light unevenly, creating a soft effect. Late 18th and most 19th century glazes are higher in their shine but fall short of the glassy effect of modern ceramics. Those pieces decorated with Hirado patterns and having a very high gloss finish are likely to have been made in the very last years of Hirado production or they may be copies from another kiln. A third possibility is that they are modern copies.

PASTE

It is the paste of the body itself that is the most consistent factor in Hirado's

141

production. The Amakusa clay is white, showing none of the slightly yellowish tint seen in the clay used at the Arita kilns. It is important when studying the paste of the body that only unglazed areas be used. The appearance of the clay is different when seen through glaze. This generally means studying the small unglazed portion of the footring. Of course, footrings are often discoloured by dirt over the years and it is important to distinguish between a dirty paste and the true colour of the original body material. Should this be difficult to determine no harm will come to the piece by immersing it in water with detergent and scrubbing the foot rim with a brush. A word of caution: pieces with repair should not be treated in this way, as cleaning may discolour or remove the restoration.

To make the finest pieces and achieve the whitest of white body colour, the potters would refine and purify the Amakusa clay to an extreme degree. The clay used in making lesser pieces was not treated to such an extent and consequently is slightly less white and less dense. Porcelain from the purest clay is extremely dense and, when the walls of a jar or vase are thickly potted, they are very heavy, in fact, noticeably heavier than comparable pieces made at other kilns. This density leads to a paste that is exceptionally smooth; running a finger over the unglazed part of a foot rim and comparing this to an Arita piece is often the

best indicator that a piece has its origin at the Mikawachi kilns.

The Amakusa clay has a slight tendency to tear during the firing process and small fissures up to 5 cms long can sometimes be found on the body of Hirado wares. These firing flaws differ from pieces using Izumiyama clay in that they retain their sharp edges underneath the glaze whereas Arita firing flaws·generally become a simple rough-edged crack.

DESIGN

What kind of object is it? It is important to consider this basic element as a surprising amount of insight can be gained by this. Is it something only of use in the West? Then, if Hirado, it *must* be 19th century at the earliest and most probably late in the century. Is it for use in Japan? For tea ceremony? Then it *could* have been made for the Matsura and *could* date as far back as the origins of the kiln. Is it very large or small? Big Hirado pieces (over 25 cms) were not made in the 18th century, so it must be later. By asking oneself a series of essentially simple questions, the possibilities can be narrowed substantially.

Establishing dates within the 19th century is the most common problem and one of the most difficult to solve. This book has attempted to establish that items produced in the early 19th century were made for the

Matsura family (aside from eggshell tablewares made for export). An item that purports to be from this era must be in the taste of the time. It cannot be elaborately embellished or be decorated with a conglomeration of unrelated themes as such items did not come into fashion until the beginning of the Meiji era. That is not to say simpler objects *must* be from the Edo period. In general, after the initial impact of Western taste on Japanese applied art in the early years of Meiji, a reversion to simpler forms occurred, once again reflecting the traditional Japanese aesthetic.

COLOUR

The earliest Hirado wares are painted with a strong, rugged, darkish blue. By the early 18th century this has been replaced by a softer, subtler blue that allowed the painter to make full use of the range of shades available. However it is difficult to pinpoint a specific blue colour that would identify 19th century pieces as such a wide range of colours were employed at different times. The Hirado decorators were always trying to create a colour that is of a softer, gentler appeal than the Chinese Ming original that inspired much of the production. In addition there is always the difficulty of achieving the desired effect in practice. Misfired pieces, generally of a rich dark colour, show signs of overfiring; a tendency of the colour to turn grey or even black in parts. This is often found on Hirado as indeed are pieces that

are blurred, the colour spreading into the body after it has been applied, sometimes making it difficult to see the full intention of the design.

MARKS

The vast majority of Hirado porcelains are not marked and the lack of mark does not in any way artistically diminish the piece. Most common among the marks seen are those that say Hirado or Mikawachi followed by an artists or potters name. Occasionally other longer marks are found either with a dedication or date and it is to these that one can look for useful information, both related to the piece itself and to further understanding of Hirado as a whole. There were very few marks used in the 18th century; only those listed in appendices 3 and 6 have been recorded so far. Any marked piece is likely to date from the 19th century. A mark is a strong guarantee that the piece is really from Hirado, providing this supported by the nature of the piece itself and so some measure of comfort may be found in that fact. Although the date of an object is interesting, and very important on occasions, it should not be taken as the primary reason for acquiring Hirado. The criteria that, I believe, should be applied relate to quality and collectors of Hirado are in the fortunate position of knowing that within his or her chosen field are some of the finest ceramics made.

Marks on Hirado porcelain

This list includes most signatures so far known as well as a selection of location and other marks found on Hirado wares. Japanese names can often be read in more than one way. The readings offered here are those that have found general acceptance but alternative readings may be possible.

Marks are in underglaze blue unless otherwise stated.

Signatures and marks on Hirado ceramics. Commas have been added in the transcriptions to indicate breaks between lines.

大	dai	great
平戸	Hirado	[place name]
筆	hitsu	painted
之	kore/no	this/possessive particle
三川内	Mikawachi	[place name]
日本	Nihon	Japan
作	saku	made
産	san	product (of)
製	sei	manufactured
造	tsukuru	made
燒	yaki	ware

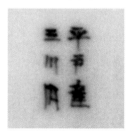

1

Hirado san,
Mikawachi

2

Hirado san,
Mikawachi

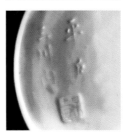

3

Hirado san,
Mikawachi,
Nakanaga sei

4

Hirado san,
Mikawachi,
Imasuke sei
(incised)

5

Hirado san,
Mikawachi,
Imasuke sei
(incised)

6

Hirado,
Mikawachi,
Nihon to
[Japan ceramics]
(in relief)

7

Hirado,
Mikawachi-yama,
Imamura Ryosaku
kore o tsukuru
(incised)

145

8

Hirado Mikawachi Sarayama, Imamura Ryosaku kore o tsukuru (incised)

9

Hirado, Mataemon, saku (incised)

10

Hirado, sho

11

Hirado, Ryozan, with kakihan

12

Hirado, kasho ["good omen"]

13

Hirado, Gasho
(see no.37)

14

Hirado sei

15

Hirado sei

16

Hirado, sei sei

17

Hirado san,
Giei tsukuru
(compare no.100)

Kogo with butterfly, Baur coll. E 78

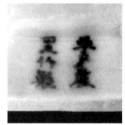
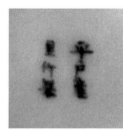

18

Hirado san,
Satomi sei

19

Hirado san,
Richiku sei

20

Hirado san,
Richiku sei

21

Hirado san,
Mikawachi-mura,
Imamura
Bunkichi

22

Hirado Goemon
saku
(incised)

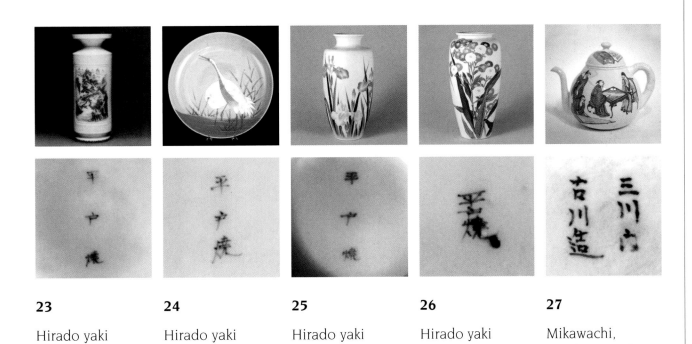

23

Hirado yaki

24

Hirado yaki

25

Hirado yaki

26

Hirado yaki

27

Mikawachi,
Furukawa tsukuru
(black on
unglazed base)

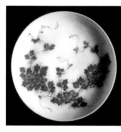

Bottle, pine decoration

28

Dai Nihon, Mikawachi, Furukawa sei

29

Hirado Mikawachi, Satomi Katsushige, ?? Nobutaka, kore o sei

|Hirado Mikawachi, Satomi Katsushige and ?? Nobutaka made this| (incised) (lacquered vase)

30

Hirado Mikawachi, Imamura Yajibei, sei

31

Mikawachi Kobun (impressed)

32

Mikawachi, Yamoto tsukuru (incised)

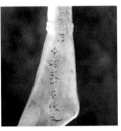

33

Mikawachi,
Imakatsu sei

34

Mikawachi,
Imamura Bunjuro
kore o saku
(incised)

35

Mikawachi,
Imamura Bunjuro
kore o saku
(incised)

36

Mikawachi,
Imajika sei
(impressed)

(underglaze grey
and blue)

37

Mikawachi, Gasho
sei
(see no.13)

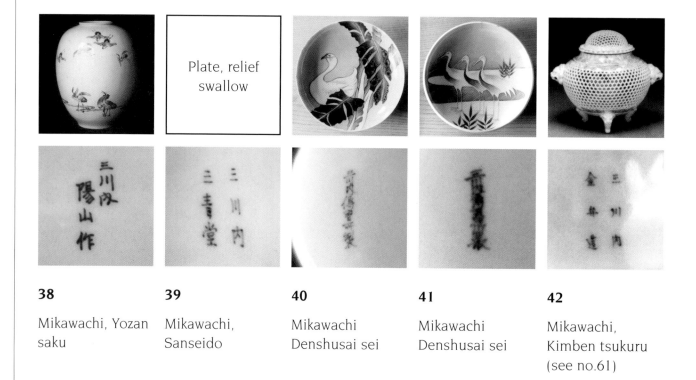

三川内
陽山作

三川内
三青堂

三川内信雲研究

三川内信雲研究

三川内
金弁造

38

Mikawachi, Yozan
saku

39

Mikawachi,
Sanseido

40

Mikawachi
Denshusai sei

41

Mikawachi
Denshusai sei

42

Mikawachi,
Kimben tsukuru
(see no.61)

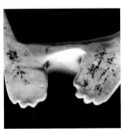
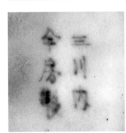
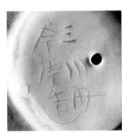

43

Mikawachi,
Komarujo tsukuru

|made by the
woman Komaru|
(incised)

44

?? Mikawachi, ??
Chikamitsu,
Hoei ni |1705|

|the date is
probably
spurious|

45

Mikawachi,
Imabo sei

|Imabo is a
contraction of
Imamura kobo,
meaning
"Imamura's
workshop"|

46

Mikawachi, Imabo
tsukuru
(incised)
(see no.45)

47

Mikawachi,
Goshigaisha
|Limited
company| sei

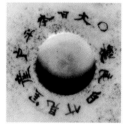
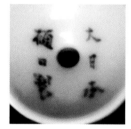

48

Dai Nihon,
Hirado san

49

Dai Nihon Hirado
san Satomi
Takeshiro sei

50

Dai Nihon,
Higuchi sei

51

Dai Nihon,
Kuchiishi tei,
Mikawachi
(incised)

52

Dai Nihon
Mikawachi,
Nakazato
Magosaburo sei

Plate with shishi

53

?? Yakuji
[in time of
trouble] Mishima,
Hirado ?? sei

54

Ei
(black on
unglazed bare)

55

Sanko
(impressed)

56

Toyojima sei

57

Seizando, Ryuo,
Minamoto ?
(incised and
impressed)

58

Moemon, below
a Matsura three-
star mon
(impressed and
incised)

59

Masatami
(incised)

60

Masakazu
(impressed)

61

Kimben tsukuru
(see no.42)

62

Tempo hitsuji
chushu,
Mikawachi sei,
Wakigawa kore o
tsutaeru

|Made at
Mikawachi in
mid-autumn of
the sheep year of
the Tempo era
|1835| to be
handed down in
the Wakigawa
family|

(see nos.84–5,
87–8)

63

Kaei go, ne hachigatsu kichinichi, Fukubei

[Made by Fukubei on a lucky day in the eighth month of the fifth, rat, year of Kaei [1852]]

64

Kyushu Hizen Hirado, Yamaguchi-shi, Ansei rokusai, hitsuji rokugatsu kichinichi

[Made for Mr Yamaguchi at Hirado in Hizen province, Kyushu, on a lucky day in the sixth month of the sixth, sheep, year of Ansei [1859]]

65

(front)
Bunsei ni mi sai, hokenjo, yashiki, rokugatsu kisshojitsu

(reverse)
Fukumoto Heijiro

[Presented at the Residence on an auspicious day of the sixth month of the second, snake, year of Bunsei [1819]]
(The snake year was in fact 1821)

66

(in low relief)

67

mokko mon

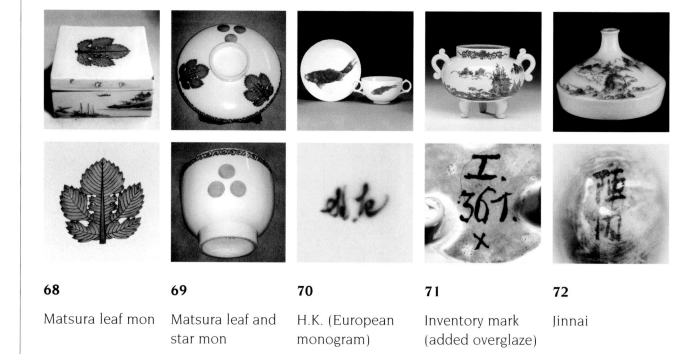

68

Matsura leaf mon

69

Matsura leaf and
star mon

70

H.K. (European
monogram)

71

Inventory mark
(added overglaze)

72

Jinnai

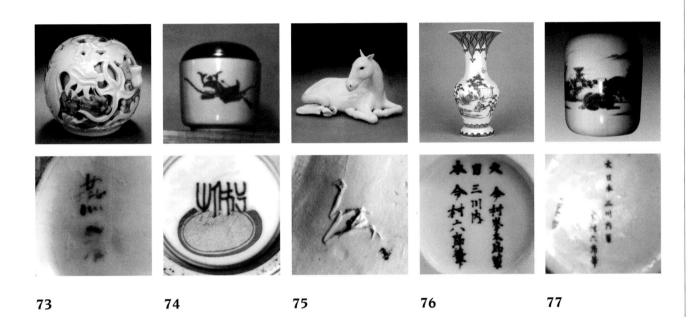

73

Tsubame ? saku

74

Sonsen

75

Unread
(incised)

76

Dai Nihon,
Imamura Hotaro
sei, Mikawachi,
Imamura Rokuro
hitsu

77

Dai Nihon
Mikawachi sei,
Imamura Rokuro
hitsu

Large vase with
pine tree

78

Dai Nihon, Hirado,
Furukawa Einojo
tsukuru, Mikawachi,
Nakazato Shigota
hitsu

79

Dai Nihon, Nagasaki-
ken, Mikawachi,
Satomi Takeshiro

80

Dai Nihon naikoku,
kangyo hakurankai,
santo-sho Mikawachi,
Nakazato Shigota sei

[Made by Nakazato
Shigota of Mikawachi
as third prize at the
National Industrial
Exposition]

(This Exposition was
held in 1903)

81

Kobe
Sanjurokubankan,
Deyasu shokai no,
chumon ni yori kore o,
seisu, Mikawachi
Toyojima

[Made by Toyojima of
Mikawachi to the order
of the Deyasu Trading
Company of the
Sanjurokubankan
Building in Kobe]

82

Hono Hizen Hirado, Matsura Hizen no kami uchi, Tamaokiyama Makiyama-shi Enrin, Kyoho hachinen u

[Dedicated on behalf of Hirado Matsura, Lord of Hizen Province, by Mr. Makiyama Enrin of Tamaokiyama in the eighth, hare, year of Kyoho [1723]]

83

An'ei nen Shukosha no motome ni ojite, sei Tsuji Hitachi no daijo aijo

[Made for the lasting delight Tsuji, Lord of Hitachi Province, to the order of the Shukosha Company during the An'ei period [1772–81]]

84

Tempo roku kinoto-hitsuji shoto chujun, Mikawachi onzaikudokoro ni oite, Kuchiishi Kamesaburo kore o saku, Wakigawa Seisaku keishi motsu

[Made by Kuchiishi Kamesaburo at the craft workshops in Mikawachi in the middle of the tenth month of the sixth, kinoto-hitsuji, year of Tempo [1835]; owned with great pleasure by Wakigawa Seisaku]

(The underside of the lid is marked, it may be that the lid and base do not match.)

85

Mikawachi sei, Tempo roku kinoto-hitsuji toshi, Wakigawa-ke ni tsutaeru

[Made at Mikawachi in the sixth, kinoto-hitsuji, year of Tempo [1835]; to be passed down in the Wakigawa family]

161

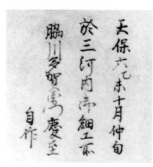

86

Tempo roku kinoto-hitsuji sai goyoshogama, gaho Imamura Riemon, rokuro Kuchiishi Yohei

[Made at the official kiln in sixth, kinoto-hitsuji, year of Tempo [1835]; painter Imamura Riemon, potter Kuchiishi Yohei]

87

Tempo roku kinoto-hitsuji jugatsu chujun, Mikawachi onzaikudokoro ni oite, Wakigawa Tagaemon keishi, jisaku

[Made for pleasure by Wakigawa Tagaemon at the craft workshops in Mikawachi in the middle of the tenth month of the sixth, kinoto-hitsuji, year of Tempo [1835]]

88

Tempo shichi saru sai, Hirado Mikawachi onzaikudokoro sei, Wakigawa keishi choki

[A utensil supplied for the pleasure of Mr Wakigawa at the craft workshops in Mikawachi, Hirado, in the seventh, kinoto-hitsuji, year of Tempo [1836]]

89

Kaei roku mizunoto-ushi, shoka no hi, Imamura Riemon, Masanori (kakihan), rokujugosai, kore o ga

[This was painted at the age of 65 by Imamura Riemon Masanori on a summer day in the sixth, mizunoto-ushi, year of Kaei [1853]]

**Marks on overglaze
decorated Hirado**

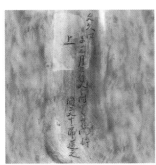

90

Bunkyu yon, ne sangatsu jojun Imamura Tomiemon sui, jo, do Bunjuro kore o tsukuru

|Specially made by Imamura Tomiemon and Imamura Bunjuro in the first part of the third month of the fourth, rat, year of Bunkyu |1864|. Presented.| (incised)

91

Genji ni gogatsu, juhachinichi yotsudoki ?, ? ni oite, Wakasaburo ?

|Wakasaburo ?, at the fourth hour of the eighteenth day of the fifth month of the second of Genji |1865||

92

Dai Nihon Mikawachi sei (impressed), Koransha ni oite, Nishiyama sei (red overglaze)

93

Fukagawa Fuji mark (overglaze)

163

94

Fukagawa sei,
below Fuji mark
(underglaze blue)

95

Keimei with seal
(overglaze)

96

Zoshuntei,
Sampo sei
(overglaze)

97

Hirado,
Mikawachi sei
(overglaze)

98

Hichozan,
Shimpo tsukuru
(overglaze)

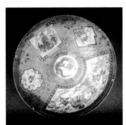

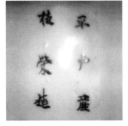

99

Mikawachi,
Shinryoku tsukuru
with Koransha
trademark.
(red and gold
overglaze

100

Hirado san,
Giei tsukuru
(red overglaze)
(compare no.17)

101

Dai Nihon,
Hirado san,
Shinryoku sei
(red overglaze)

Extract from the Manchester Guardian 1891

The high level of excellence attained in Japanese pottery is not, however, due entirely to her potters, but in the past to the wise and powerful patronage of her great nobles. To own a small pottery from which special articles could be turned out to be used as gifts was the pride and pleasure of many of the old Daimios, such as the Prince of Matsura and the Prince of Satsuma. The porcelain made under the patronage of the Matsura family is known as Hirato, from the east of the factory. It was established more than 700 years ago, and the finest pieces were used as gifts from the Prince of Matsura to the Shogun and others, and their sale was forbidden. The clay is peculiarly fine and white. The most valued pieces are painted under the glaze, and represent the subject of Chinese boys playing under a pine tree. On the ware of the best quality seven boys are painted, and on the less valuable five or only three are given. Of modern Hirato the best known examples are exquisite little figures modelled to perfection in the finest pocelain, or vases and jars, with raised flowers, such as sprays of hawthorn blossom, delicately chiselled in the clay. Delightful specimens of this ware are in the private collectons of Mr. Lowder at Yokohama and Captain Brinkley at Tokio. Knowing the traditions and beauty of this ware, it was to us a delightful surprise one day, when calling upon Count Matsura at Tokio, to find that he still acted as patron of the porcelain which owes its existence to his family, and that in a corner of his garden, which is known as one of the most beautiful and extensive in Tokio, a potter is to be found at work throwing on the wheel and modelling with his hands dainty specimens of white Hirato, to be used as gifts to royal and distinguished persons. Little statuettes destined to be presented to the King and Queen of Greece were in process of manufacture, and we had the pleasure of seeing the potter throw on the wheel and model three vases, which received our initials before going to the oven to be baked, and given us by Count Matsura as a memento of our pleasant and interesting visit.

The author would like to acknowledge with thanks the following persons and organisations for the use of the following photographs:

Philip Cardeiro 77, 83 & 84

Flying Cranes Antiques Ltd 53, 57, 73 & 99

Dresden Porcelain Collection 24

Paul Freeman 16 & 40

Michael Goedhuis 54

Kenneth and Mary Izzo 37, 43, 58, 66, 69 & 78 Photographed by David S. Lightner

David Hyatt King 1, 18, 25, 29, 60, 61, 71, 92, 98, 100

Louis Lawrence Ltd 2, 6, 7, 9, 10, 13, 14, 15, 19, 20, 21, 22, 23, 30, 33, 34, 35, 36, 38, 39, 41, 42, 44, 45, 47, 52, 55, 56, 59, 63–65, 67, 68, 70, 72, 74, 75, 76, 79, 85, 86, 88, 89, 90, 93, 94, 95, 97, 101 & cover.

Mr Matsura Akira 3, 4, 8, 48–51

The Metropolitan Museum of Art, New York 27, 28 & 91

The National Museum of Ethnology, Leiden 32

Dr. T. Noda 5, 11 & 12

The Trustees of the National Museums of Scotland 31

Sagemonoya (Yabane Co. Ltd.—Tokyo) 80–82

F. S. Shimizu 87

Private collections 17, 26, 46, 62 & 96

Location of illustrated examples, when known

MAIN TEXT

Cover The Kurtzman family collection

1. Hyatt King collection

9. The author

10. The Kurtzman family collection

13. The author

16. Paul Freeman

17. The late Soame Jenyns collection

18. Hyatt King collection

20. The author

22. The author

24. Dresden Porcelain collection

25. Hyatt King collection

27. The Metropolitan Museum of Art

28. The Metropolitan Museum of Art

29. Hyatt King Collection, loan to the Victoria and Albert Museum

30. The author

31. The Royal Scottish Museum, Edinburgh

32. The National Museum of Ethnography, Leiden

35. The author

37. Ken and Mary Izzo collection

38. Ken and Mary Izzo collection

39. The Silva collection

40. Paul Freeman

41. The author

42. The British Museum

43. Ken and Mary Izzo collection

44. The Kurtzman family collection

48–51. Matsura private collection

52. The author

53. Flying Cranes Antiques Ltd

57. Flying Cranes Antiques Ltd

58. Ken and Mary Izzo collection

59. Ken and Mary Izzo collection

60. Hyatt King collection

61. Hyatt King collection

63. The author

66. Ken and Mary Izzo collection

67. The author

68. The author

69. Ken and Mary Izzo collection

70. Ken and Mary Izzo collection

71. Hyatt King collection

72. The author

73. Flying Cranes Antiques Ltd

74. The Kurtzman family collection

75. The Kurtzman family collection

77. Cardeiro collection

78. Ken and Mary Izzo collection

79. The Kurtzman family collection

83 & 84. Cardeiro collection

85. The Kurtzman family collection

86. Ken and Mary Izzo collection

87. Hyatt King collection

88. Ken and Mary Izzo collection

89. The Kurtzman family collection

90. Ken and Mary Izzo collection

91. The Metropolitan Museum of Art

92. Hyatt King collection

95. The Kurtzman family collection

97. Ken and Mary Izzo collection

98. Hyatt King collection

99. Flying Cranes Antiques Ltd.

100. Hyatt King collection

101. Ken and Mary Izzo collection

APPENDIX 6

2. Cardeiro collection

4. Flying Cranes Antiques Ltd

6. Hyatt King collection

7. Hyatt King collection

8. The Kurtzman family collection

9. The author

10 & 11. Ken and Mary Izzo collection

12. The British Museum

13. Cardeiro collection

14. The Walters Art Gallery

15. The Victoria and Albert Museum

16. Hyatt King collection

17. The author

19. Hyatt King collection

20. Hyatt King collection

21. The British Museum

22. Baur collection

24. Cardeiro collection

25. Ken and Mary Izzo collection

26. The Kurtzman family collection

28. Silva collection

29. Hyatt King collection

30. The British Museum

32. Hyatt King collection

33. Hyatt King collection

34. Ahearn collection

35. The British Museum
36. The Kurtzman family collection
37. The Ashmolean Museum, Oxford
38. Silva collection
39. The Kurtzman family collection
40. Hyatt King collection
41. Hyatt King collection
42. Ken and Mary Izzo collection
43. Hyatt King collection
44. The Kurtzman family collection
46. The Kurtzman family collection
47. Hyatt King collection
48. Flying Cranes Antiques Ltd
49. The Kurtzman family collection
50. Hyatt King collection
51. The British Museum
52. The British Museum
53. The Kurtzman family collection
54. The Kurtzman family collection
55. The British Museum
56. Hyatt King collection
57. Hyatt King collection
58. The Kurtzman family collection
59. The Kurtzman family collection
60. Hyatt King collection
61. The British Museum

66. The Kurtzman family collection
68. Musee Guimet, Paris
69. The Walters Art Gallery, Baltimore
70. Paul Freeman
71. Dresden Porcelain collection
72. Cardeiro collection
73. The Kurtzman family collection
74. The Walters Art Gallery, Baltimore
75. The Kurtzman family collection
76. Hyatt King collection
78. Hyatt King collection
79. Hyatt King collection
81. Hyatt King collection
83. Hyatt King collection
86. Hyatt King collection, on loan to the Victoria & Albert Museum
90. Hyatt King collection
91. The Kurtzman family collection
92. The Victoria & Albert Museum
93. Hyatt King collection
94. The British Museum
95. Hyatt King Collection
99. The Victoria & Albert Museum
101. M.C.N. Antiques

Bibliography

IN ENGLISH

Ayres, John, *The Baur Collection, Geneva; Japanese Ceramics* (Geneva, 1982)

Beasley, W.G., *The Modern History of Japan* (London, 1973)

Brinkley, Captain F., *Japan: Its History Arts and Literature* (Boston, 1901)

Bushell, Stephen W., *Oriental Ceramic Art* (London, 1896)

Cardeiro, C. Philip, *Hirado Ware* (Monterey, 1989)

Cleveland, Richard, *200 Years of Japanese Porcelain* (St. Louis, 1970)

Davey, Neil K., *Netsuke: A comprehensive study based on the M.T. Hindson Collection* (London, 1974)

Earle, Joe, *Flower Bronzes of Japan,* (London, 1995)

Emerson-Dell, Kathleen, *Bridging East and West: Japanese Ceramics from the Kozan Studio* (Baltimore, 1994)

Ford, Barbara, and Impey, Oliver, *Japanese Art from the Gerry Collection in the Metropolitan Museum of Art* (New York, 1989)

Franks, Sir Augustus W., *Japanese Pottery* (London, 1906)

Garner, H.M., *Oriental Blue and White* (London, 1954)

Guth, Christine M.E., *Art, Tea, and Industry* (Princeton, 1993)

Hinton, Mark, and Impey, Oliver, *Kakiemon Porcelain from the English Country House* (Oxford, 1989)

Impey, Oliver, and Mallet, J.V.G., *Porcelain for Palaces: The Fashion for Japan, 1650–1750* (London, 1990)

[Impey, Oliver and Fairley, Malcolm] *Treasures of Imperial Japan. The Nasser D. Khalili Collection of Japanese Art, V: Ceramics Part I,* (London, 1995)

Impey, Oliver, *The Early Porcelain Kilns of Japan: Arita in the First Half of the Seventeenth Century* (Oxford, 1996)

[Jenyns, Soame] The Oriental Ceramic Society, catalogue of, *A Loan Exhibition of Japanese Porcelain* (London, 1965)

Jenyns, Soame, *Japanese Porcelain* (London, 1965)

King, David Hyatt, *Transactions of the Oriental Ceramic Society.Hirado Porcelain: Its Dating* (London, 1981)

King, David Hyatt, Andon 30 vol 8/2, *Early 19th Century Porcelain Netsuke in the National Museum of Ethnology, Leiden* (Holland, 1988)

Lane, Richard, *Hokusai: Life and Work* (London, 1989)

Lawrence, Louis, *Hirado Porcelain* Exhibition Catalogue, (London, 1981)

Lawrence, Louis, *Satsuma: Masterpieces from the World's Important Collections* (London, 1991)

Lawrence, Louis, *Hirado: A Prince among Porcelains*, Catalogue of the Arts of Pacific Asia Show, (San Francisco, 1994)

Nagatake, T, Hayashi, S & Nishida, H, *Art of World Ceramics*, vol 8 (Tokyo, 1978)

Rein, J.J., *The Industries of Japan* (New York, 1889)

[Shimizu, Yoshiaki], *Japan: The Shaping of Daimyo Culture* (London, 1989)

Smith, Lawrence, *Transactions of the Oriental Ceramic Society. Japanese Porcelain in the first half of the Nineteenth Century*, (London, 1973)

——————————, *Assignment Japan: von Siebold, Pioneer and Collector* (The Hague, 1989)

——————————, *Meiji: Japanese Art in Transition* (Leiden, 1987)

——————————, *Shadowed Reflections, Japanese Views*. A catalogue by Kagedo Japanese Art, (Seattle, 1997)

IN JAPANESE

Noda, Toshio, Dr., *Hizen Hirado yaki Dokohon* (Japan, 1989)

Noda, Toshio, Dr., *Miwaka no ko-Hirado yaki* (Japan, 1993)

Seki, Kazuo, *Beauty of Prime Period Imari* (Japan, 1990)

Yamaguchi, M, *Hirado yaki Kai-ku* (Osaka, 1979)

——————————, *catalogue of the Tokyo Bijitsu Club auction of the Matsura family collection* (Tokyo, 1928)

——————————, *catalogue of the Tokyo Bijitsu Club auction of the Matsura family collection* (Tokyo, 1935)

——————————, *Imamura clan records* (unpublished)

——————————, *Matsura family documents* (unpublished)

——————————, *Kyoto Prefectural Museum Report on Mikawachi Porcelain* (Kyoto, 1882)

——————————, *Chiisani tsubomi*, vol 241 (Japan, 1993)

——————————, *Nagasaki-no-Toji Tokubetsuten* (Japan, 1989)

——————————, *Sasebo City Educational Committee report* (Japan, 1983)

Index